"*Refresh! - a Spa for Your Soul* is like a [barcode] day. With her usual bottom-line honesty, author Cindy Secrest McDowell helps her readers to understand the importance of taking time for personal renewal, physical rest, and spiritual replenishment. Your mind and heart will be revitalized with key quotes, biblical insights, and practical applications. This is a book for women like me who are worn out! Buy one for yourself and ten more to give away!"

Carol Kent, Best-selling author
Becoming a Woman of Influence

"Dive into *Refresh!* This refreshing makeover for your soul sparkles with personal insights from Cindy. Enjoy!"

Robin Jones Gunn, Best-selling author
Sisterchicks fiction series

"You are going to love *Refresh!* Cindy's transparency made this book so real that I relished every word. I totally agree that 'the best spa for your soul is one in which God heals and massages and cleanses and beautifies from the inside out.' The reader is left wanting God to do just that in her own life."

Carole Lewis, First Place 4 Health Director emeritus and author
A Thankful Heart

"*Refresh!* is a catalyst for real change and renewal. If you are sick and tired of being sick and tired, then Cindy's words will be as comforting to your heart and life as those plush white spa robes are to your body! I recommend *Refresh!* for every woman who longs for a fresh start or hope for her weary heart and body."

Pam Farrel, Best-Selling Author
7 Simple Skills for Every Woman

"*Refresh!* provides a fabulous companion for the joy of pampering your body while pondering soul matters. This is a fabulous 'come away' book that will give you an excuse to luxuriate your body while rejuvenating your spirit."

Ellie Kay, Best-Selling Author
Lean Body, Fat Wallet

"More than ever, we women need to tend to our souls, care for our bodies, and allow God to make us into the women we were created to be. Book an appointment with Cindy's *Refresh!* You'll feel cleaned, rejuvenated, and loved!"

Nancy Stafford, Actress and Author
Beauty by the Book and *The Wonder of His Love*

"With her characteristic inspiration, wit and creative ideas, Cindy McDowell will refresh and renew your heart, mind, spirit (and body too) in her new book *Refresh! - a Spa for Your Soul.*"

Cheri Fuller, Best-selling author
What a Girl Needs from Her Mom

refresh!

a spa *for your* soul

For Karen –
May the Lord
refresh you
Psalm 62.5

Lucinda Secrest McDowell

Lucinda Secrest McDowell

BVB

**Dedicated to my husband,
T. Michael McDowell**

*Thank you for being such
a faithful example of one
who daily cultivates his
inner life with God and
encourages me to make
my own "soul care"
a priority as well.*

Contents

Heart that is frozen - a handful of snow,
Heart that is faded - a sky without glow,
Come unto Me, and I will refresh you.

Heart that is weary, O come unto Me.
Fear not, whatever the trouble may be;
Come unto Me, and I will refresh you.

~ Amy Carmichael 1867-1951

Beside Still Waters

"He leads me beside still waters. He restores my soul."
—Psalm 23:2,3 NIV

A salty breeze blew through my hair as I descended the rustic staircase from the overlook down to the pink sand beach below. It was early morning and I seemed to be the only person awake to this fresh new day. Making my way to a favorite chair, I unloaded my prayer book and journal and settled down with a sigh.

Immediately the psalmist's words came to me, "Be still and know that I am God." (Psalm 46:10) Another deep breath, this time with closed eyes. I wanted to literally soak it all in and not miss a single sensation that God had for me. Even though I was in Bermuda to lead a "Spa for the Soul" retreat at one of my favorite places in the world — *Willowbank* — I sensed that God also had some refreshing plans for my own soul during my stay.

What do you think of when you hear the word "spa?" A fancy resort complete with hovering attendants eager to pamper you with massage therapy, a body scrub and sauna? Or perhaps you're reminded of that elaborate hot tub at your friends' vacation home, complete with jets of soothing water? Maybe your local beauty salon has just changed its name to "Day Spa" and you can now finally afford such 'luxuries' as a pedicure or facial?

Whatever your mental image of spa, it probably involves images of serenity, rest and perhaps water. Spa is a word that is actually an acronym for three Latin words – *Salus Per Aquam,* which mean "health by water." While water is the genesis of this term, health is an integral ingredient. Any true spa will focus on improving your health — physically, emotionally, mentally and yes, spiritually. Modern spas have their roots in the ancient towns once known for the healing powers of their mineral waters and hot springs. People would come from far away to "take the waters" and restore their health. In the Bible, the Pool of Bethesda was such a spa and believed to be a source of healing when the waters were stirred. That's why the lame man had waited by that pool for 38 years, hoping to 'take the waters.' (more about this story in chapter 6)

As much as I love receiving a good massage or having a pedicure, I realize such treatments only satisfy for awhile – my muscles eventually tense up again and my heels get rough and calloused. What I really need is a spa for my soul — refreshing water to quench my deepest thirst. The world's cares and concerns have plopped me in the middle of a desert and I'm dry and dusty just like the psalmist who lamented, "God, You are my God; I eagerly seek You. I thirst for You; my body faints for You in a land that is dry, desolate, and without water." (Psalm 63:1)

Do you need to be refreshed?

We twenty-first century folk are not unlike those we read of long ago who also turned to God during desert moments. "Some wandered in the desolate wilderness, finding no way to a city where they could live. They were hungry and thirsty; their spirits failed within them. Then they cried out to the LORD in their trouble; He rescued them from their distress. He led them by the right path to go to a city where they could live. Let them give thanks to the LORD for His faithful love and His wonderful works for the human race. For He has satisfied the thirsty and filled the hungry with good things... He turns a desert into a pool of water, dry land into springs of water." (Psalm 107:4-9, 35)

Do you have a dehydrated heart? When our bodies lack water they give off symptoms of dehydration such as dry mouth, headaches or weak knees. Physically we cannot survive without water for numerous functions: we need moisture to swallow, sweat to keep cool, blood to carry cells, and fluid to cry and cleanse our eyes. Thirst is our built-in indicator that there is a need.

But what are the indicators that our souls are deprived of spiritual water? "Dehydrated hearts send desperate messages. Snarling tempers. Waves of worry. Growling mastodons of guilt and fear. You think God wants you to live with these? Hopelessness. Sleeplessness. Loneliness. Resentment. Irritability. Insecurity. These are warnings. Symptoms of a dryness deep within."[1]

What is needed is 'health by water' — a spa for our souls! And it must come from the Source of living water — Jesus Christ!

Recently I had the privilege of being at the Water Gate in Old Jerusalem. By simply closing my eyes, I could picture back to thousands of years ago when the priests walked to the temple through the Water Gate with a filled pitcher as the crowds recounted the prophet's words, "You will joyfully draw water from the springs of salvation." (Isaiah 12:3) Perhaps it was at that very moment as the priest poured the water on the altar that the controversial Teacher from Nazareth stood and literally shouted, "If anyone is thirsty, he should come to Me and drink! The one who believes in Me, as the Scripture has said, will have streams of living water flow from deep within him." (John 7:37-38) It's hard for us to imagine what a truly radical act this was as Jesus completely bypassed religious ritual and offered the dry and weary throngs a provision for their deepest need.

He made a similar offer to the woman at the well in Samaria. Now here was someone who had camped out in a desert place for many years, hoping each new encounter would finally assuage the dryness of her heart — only to come away more parched than before. That morning she had come early to the well hoping to get her liquid allotment without encountering any of the townspeople.

But Jesus offered her a spa for her soul and body..."Everyone who drinks from this water will get thirsty again. But whoever drinks from the water that I will give him will never get thirsty again—ever! In fact, the water I will give him will become a well of water springing up within him for eternal life." (John 4:13-14)

Sitting on my favorite Bermuda beach that morning I prayed, *"Lord, I thirst. I'm dry and discouraged. Pour over me your living water. May I drink deeply of You so that out of me will truly flow a wellspring of life for others! Amen."* Then I sang (quietly so as not to disturb others) words from Charles Wesley's 1740 hymn "Jesus, Lover of My Soul."

> *"Plenteous grace with Thee is found, grace to cover all my sin;*
> *Let the healing streams abound; make and keep me pure within.*
> *Thou of life the fountain art, freely let me drink of Thee;*
> *Spring Thou up within my heart; rise to all eternity."*

God has made each of us in His image — body and soul. When we neglect one part, the other suffers. I have learned this the hard way. There have been seasons in my life when I focused on the spiritual, while unwittingly neglecting my physical health. There have been other seasons when the outward seemed to get more attention from me than the inward. In both instances, my life was out of balance and needed restoration.

This book, *Refresh!* is part of my journey which I offer to you as a tool for examining areas of balance in your own life. I'm still very much a fellow traveler along the way and haven't mastered all disciplines completely. But, my prayer for both of us is that we drink deeply of that living water that Jesus off ers. You, too, can experience a refreshing – SPA – as you walk through each chapter and do your own **S**piritual **P**ersonal **A**ssessment activities.

"Come everyone who is thirsty. Come to the waters...
Seek the Lord while He may be found. Call to Him while He is near."

—Isaiah 55:1-6

CHAPTER 1

Come Apart Awhile

"Here's what I want you to do: Find a quiet, secluded place
so you won't be tempted to role-play before God.
Just be there as simply and honestly as you can manage.
The focus will shift from you to God, and you will begin to sense his grace."
—Matthew 6:6 MSG

I was cold and the day was colder. January days in New England mean dirty snow and gray skies. I'd been fighting a bronchial infection for weeks, and our family was still mourning the recent loss of my beloved mother-in-law and our children's grandmother. So I wasn't surprised when the newspaper ad seemed to jump off the page and into my heart—"Personal Spa Day" at the Spa at Norwich Inn, about an hour away. During the off-season, when most of their spa clientele were playing snowbird in Florida, this renowned spa offered a deeply discounted rate, which included two spa treatments, use of all facilities, and lunch. What a deal! I tore out the ad and placed it in my journal and on my mind's back burner to simmer awhile.

The next time my prayer group Daybreak got together, I proposed to the other three friends that because we always do something special for everyone's birthday why not try something different this year? "Let's all go together for a spa day as a birthday treat for all of us this year!" Everyone agreed, and I booked the sessions.

A whole day away in a world foreign to our frenetic lives—a world of beauty, peace, and pampering. Yes, it was a luxury, but the concept of taking time away to regroup, refresh, and refocus is something our Creator also had in mind when He commanded us, "Be still and know that I am God" (Ps. 46:10 NIV).

According to a recent *Chicago Tribune* article, "More middle-aged and older folks are keeping spa owners on their pedicured toes, as baby boomers seek to inject some serenity into their busy, frazzled lives and fight the signs of aging and poor health." While our nation's 10,000+ spas offer such physical relief, I believe more is needed to bring about a transformation in the lives of overstressed twenty-first-century Americans. We all need a spa for our *souls,* to help us grow spiritually and find emotional health and greater purpose in the remaining years of our lives.

Today the spa concept has evolved into a whole movement from "day spas," where folks can drop in for various treatments on a day-use basis, to "destination spas," where clients immerse themselves in the total experience of treatments, healthy food, exercise, medical evaluations, stress management, nutrition, education, and more.

We all need this, and more. We need rest for our souls as well as rejuvenation of our bodies. We were not created to keep going and going and going and going, like the Energizer Bunny. It's no wonder that one of our most familiar catchwords is "24/7" because that clearly describes our work week, shopping opportunities, and how often we feel we must be available to others. Yet none of us can be "on" twenty-four hours a day, seven days a week. It's simply not physically, emotionally, or spiritually possible. And when we try, we collapse.

Do you need a spa for your soul? Several different meanings of *soul* are found in the Bible, but a common understanding is that our souls comprise mind, will, and emotions. My friend Lindsey O'Connor elaborated:

The Hebrew word for soul is *nephesh*; it occurs 755 times in the Old Testament, meaning mainly "possessing life," but it also refers to the blood, the seat of physical appetite and the source of emotion. In addition, it is associated with the will and moral action of an individual, and there is some overlapping with the use of "heart" or "spirit." Paul teaches about the existence of body, soul, and spirit (1 Thess. 5:23). We see a definition of the emotional nature of the word *soul* with the verse "The soul of Jonathan was knit to the soul of David, and Jonathan loved him" (1 Sam. 18:1). Its spiritual nature is seen in Psalm 42:1–2; "As the deer pants for the water brooks, so my soul pants for You, O God. My soul thirsts for God, for the living God."[1]

Whereas most women want to go to a spa for physical refreshment, it is increasingly important to also recognize our need for spiritual renewal in the inner person, the very essence of who we are—our soul. No one knows its condition except God. Sometimes we aren't even in touch with how we're doing. But, chances are, if we are busy living one lifestyle while longing for another, then we are in great need of replenishing our souls through God's spiritual spa.

Alice Gray, coauthor of *The Worn Out Woman,* said that soul nurturing is not optional. "It's not a luxury, but a necessity. I could almost define the worn-out woman as a person who has allowed her soul to parch and wither because, for one reason or another, she has not been able to spend time beside still waters. None of us can find balance in our lives or become the women God has in mind for us to be if there is no room for the quietness that restores our souls."[2]

God ordered our lives in rhythms, and part of His creative concept was that we would take time to rest. "For the Lord GOD, the Holy One of Israel, has said: "You will be delivered by returning and resting; your strength will lie in quiet confidence. But you are not willing" (Isa. 30:15). This familiar verse comes in the context of Isaiah's admonition to the people of Judah who have rebelled against God and sought negotiations with Egypt. They are called "rebellious children" in verse 1 of Isaiah 30 because they sought advice from everyone except God.

Most Christians know that God calls us to a time of rest and meditation. We've heard the term *Sabbath* and somehow feel it isn't necessarily applicable to our lives today. And yet we also know that constant activity and overloaded lives are not satisfying our inner need to experience meaning and fulfillment in our endeavors.

Lynne Baab, in her excellent book *Sabbath Keeping*, described the Sabbath as a "weekly day of rest and worship. A day to cease working and relax in God's care for us. A day to stop the things that occupy our workdays and participate in activities that nurture peace, worship, relationships, celebration and thankfulness. The purpose of the Sabbath is to clear away the distractions of our lives so we can rest in God and experience God's grace in a new way."[3]

And yet too often we deserve this same exhortation from God: "They are a rebellious people, deceptive children, children who do not obey the LORD's instruction. They say to the seers, 'Do not see,' and to the prophets, 'Do not prophesy the truth to us. Tell us flattering things. Prophesy illusions'" (Isa. 30:9–10).

In other words, "Let me continue to live in denial!" Denial that I have physical and emotional limits. Denial that I can't really do it all. Denial that the "one day" I plan to finally focus on the things that really matter may never come. But I've lived long enough to know that if we continue to go at such a fast and furious pace, we *will* slow down. Why wait until some trauma forces you to take time for God?

The media give mixed messages. On one hand, we're told we "deserve a break today" and "it's all about me." We're wooed with every kind of luxury item imaginable, implying we're truly pampered princesses. On the other hand, we're also bombarded with reinforcements for filling every moment of our days with activity. Productivity becomes the barometer of our worth.

Too often accomplishments become the gauge of our sense of purpose and achievement. One father of two calls for dethroning this distinctly American belief. "We say, 'I don't have enough time to get it all done.' But life is not about 'getting it all done.' Life is not about filling every moment. Life is about gifts, embracing and receiving God's gifts. God may want us to be inefficient sometimes in order for us to receive His gifts more fully."[4]

> *None of us can find balance in our lives or become the women God has in mind for us to be if there is no room for the quietness that restores our souls.*
>
> —ALICE GRAY,
> *THE WORN OUT WOMAN*

Yet how can we receive God's gifts of serenity and peace unless we make deliberate decisions to order our lives around the rhythm of activity and rest? Our Lord set the example for this kind of discipline: "Very early in the morning, while it was still dark, He got up, went out, and made His way to a deserted place. And He was praying there" (Mark 1:35). In his journal of February 23, 1834, Scotsman Robert Murray M'Cheyne wrote, "Sabbath. Rose early to seek God, and found Him whom my soul loveth. Who would not rise early to meet such company?"

Who indeed? Well, I have to admit that all too often I have not risen early enough to come into the presence of God. And yet, I know that time with Him, preferably as I begin my day, provides the sustenance for all I will encounter during the remaining hours. God says six times in the book of Exodus, "I will meet with you." Imagine! The Creator and Sustainer of the universe is not only willing but *desirous* of meeting with me! When you think about it, this is staggering and humbling. His invitation is wonderfully gracious, but what will be my response? "Thanks, but no thanks, I really need to beat the crowd at the grocery store this morning." Or "There's this interview on the *Today* show I want to watch before work."

Numerous things crowd our time with the Lord. Sometimes they are valid, but often they reflect our habit of putting the urgent before the essential. In the Old Testament, God met with Moses in the Holy of Holies; but with the coming of Jesus Christ, the way was opened for all of us to meet with God and enter His presence at any time through prayer and meditation.

This then is a spiritual spa—taking time to relax in the presence of our loving God, to reflect on His goodness and His gifts, to talk to Him about all that concerns us and, more importantly, to listen carefully for that still small voice. "In solitude," Henri Nouwen wrote, "I get rid of my scaffolding. Scaffolding is all the stuff I use to keep myself propped up, to convince myself I'm important or okay. In solitude I have no friends to talk with, no phone calls or meetings, no TV to entertain, no music or books or newspapers to occupy and distract my mind. I am, in the words of the old hymn 'Just as I am': not my accomplishments or resume or possessions or networks—just me and my sinfulness, and God."[5]

Wouldn't you love to get rid of your own scaffolding? To take off the masks, set aside your title, and simply sit at the feet of Jesus *just as you are*? By taking time away from our normal responsibilities, we experience God's incredible gift of grace in a fresh way. I often describe grace as God giving us what we don't deserve and can never earn, nor can ever lose. If we really believe that grace is an undeserved gift, we can be free to stop any activity that misleads us into believing we have earned this wonderful gift of grace. By simply basking in God's love, through a time of inactivity and perhaps silence as well, we come to truly experience the assurance that we are loved apart from what we do.

That's why it's not only important to seek God's face each day through prayer, reading the Bible, and worship. It's also important to schedule periodic times of rest and reflection. A weekly sabbath is one way to do this. Also, having periodic silent retreats can truly be a spa for your soul.

During these times it is important to make deliberate decisions to cease doing what you always do in order to experience God in a fresh way.

For mothers of young children, this will definitely mean you must get away from them and from all responsibilities involved with their care. Sometimes women in your position feel guilty if you go on a retreat or a special girlfriends gathering, but this can be one of the best gifts to your family. On returning to the normal chaos and commitments, young moms feel refreshed with a new vigor and, hopefully, new spiritual encouragement to continue the great task of mothering. One of my favorite presentations when I speak at Mothers of Preschoolers (MOPS) groups is "Rest Is Not a Four-Letter Word!" The other one is "When Mama Ain't Happy, Ain't Nobody Happy!" In other words, taking care of ourselves also benefits our loved ones.

Women in midlife are also discovering the benefits of such intentional retreating. They're finding comfort and delight in experiencing silence, prayer, journaling, fasting, and enjoying nature. "In the first half of their lives, they thrived on all the abundant opportunities for fellowship and ministry offered by their churches. They are often surprised in their forties and fifties to find themselves seeking out opportunities to spend time with God in a quiet setting."[6]

Fifty years ago, Anne Morrow Lindbergh needed to get away in order to clear her mind and catch her breath. So she spent two weeks alone in a beach cottage and wrote in her journal. I'm glad she did because her book, *Gift from the Sea*, still encourages me a half century later: "My life in Connecticut, I begin to realize, lacks this quality of significance and therefore of beauty, because there is so little empty space. The space is scribbled on; the time has been filled. There are so few empty pages in my engagement pad or empty hours in the day, or empty rooms in my life in which to stand alone and find myself. Too many activities, and people and things. Too many worthy activities, valuable things and interesting people. For it is not merely the trivial which clutters our lives but the important as well. We can have a surfeit of treasures—an excess of shells, where one or two would be significant."[7]

Do you need to come apart before you fall apart? There are many ways to come apart awhile. Different experiences work at different times. Sometimes a fun gathering of girlfriends for tea and laughter and perhaps a good movie is all you need. Other times a specialized retreat or conference designed to teach and direct in specific spiritual growth is just the thing. Occasionally you need a completely silent retreat to sit at Christ's feet and soak up His love. How do you know which direction to take?

Remember those rebellious children from the book of Isaiah, those who sought advice from everyone except God? Well, perhaps a promise to them will help us as well: "He will show favor to you at the sound of your cry; when He hears, He will answer you. The Lord will give you meager bread and water during oppression, but your Teacher will not hide Himself any longer. Your eyes will see your Teacher, and whenever you turn to the right or to the left, your ears will hear this command behind you: 'This is the way. Walk in it'" (Isa. 30:19–21).

My prayer partners and I had quite a day at the spa on that winter day. Draped in our white terry cloth robes, we visited the whirlpool, the sauna, the steam room, and the swimming pool and ate a healthy lunch served in the elegant inn dining room (in which most patrons were wearing white robes and nothing else). Individually, we received body scrubs, pedicures, soothing oil massages, manicures, and makeup sessions. Believe me, you have never seen a more relaxed and pampered group than ours as we drove home!

But, of course, on our return Jessica still had to do quite a bit of troubleshooting in her management position. Karen's business responsibilities still clamored for her attention. Judy's employees and grandchildren still needed her, and I still had to finish writing this book in the midst of numerous speaking events. Nonetheless, we were glad we went. The day away not only ministered to us through the beauty and the serenity, but God spoke to our souls as well. He reminded us it's important to take time to share experiences with our sisters along the journey.

Homemaker and childbirth instructor Laura Shaffer recently discovered the benefits of periodic quiet retreats. "As with any relationship only fed by short phone calls and quick e-mails, my relationship with God suffered on a diet of mere snippets of time. Over the last few years I've gone on several silent retreats and each is different. Not every occasion yields earth-shattering, life-changing revelations. Sometimes I simply get the awesome chance to be with God, whose infinite power created the universe, and I am allowed to ponder my personal relationship with such a Savior."[8]

Saint Francis de Sales, author of the classic *An Introduction to the Devout Life*, described this need in terms of a clock. "There is no clock, no matter how good it may be, that doesn't need resetting and rewinding twice a day, once in the morning and once in the evening. In addition, at least once a year it must be taken apart to remove the dirt clogging it, straighten out bent parts, and repair those worn out. In like manner, every morning and evening a man who really takes care of his heart must rewind it for God's service. . . . At least once a year, he must take it apart and examine every piece in detail, every affection and passion, in order to repair whatever defects there may be."

So, come apart awhile. Be still and allow God's love to pour over you like healing water. "Come to Me, all of you who are weary and burdened, and I will give you rest. All of you, take up My yoke and learn from Me, because I am gentle and humble in heart, and you will find rest for yourselves" (Matt. 11:28–29).

Spiritual Personal Assessment

Scripture. Isaiah 30 tells about the people of Judah who sought advice from everyone except God. Read verses 1–2 and 9–11 and reflect on how this applies to your own actions with God. Then read what the sovereign Lord says in verses 15 and 19–22 and reflect on what He promises for those who turn to Him for rest, quietness, and trust.

Journal. Copy Matthew 6:6 printed at the beginning of this chapter. Then write down where and when you daily meet with God. What do you do during that time? Today, sit quietly in prayer and listen to the Lord. Write down what you believe He is trying to say to you. Let your pen flow through the Holy Spirit's prompting.

Discussion. What are the hindrances to your spending time apart, soaking up God's love, and finding rest for your soul? How can you overcome each one?

Do you need greater balance in your life? What needs to be pruned from your current schedule in order to carve out time for rest and spiritual restoration?

Spa Treatment. Treat yourself to a day spa or make one happen on your own. Run a hot bath filled with relaxing scented bath oil. Lock the bathroom door and put on a CD of soothing instrumental music. Light a scented candle. Put a bath pillow or rolled towel under your head and cucumber rounds on your eyes as you soak up the serenity. Enjoy!

CHAPTER 2

Deep Cleansing

He saved us—
not by works of righteousness that we had done,
but according to His mercy, through the washing
of regeneration and renewal by the Holy Spirit.
This [Spirit] He poured out on us abundantly
through Jesus Christ our Savior,
so that having been justified by His grace,
we may become heirs with the hope of eternal life.

—TITUS 3:5–7

For my birthday my dear friend gave me a gift certificate for a facial. What a luxury!

The morning of my appointment I carefully scrubbed my face so it would be clean for the aesthetician. But on my arrival, she began her work by applying a gently abrasive cleanser to my "clean" face. I was shocked to see how much dirt she removed. Surely my face was clean now, right? Hmmm. . . . Well, then a mask was applied to further remove impurities from deeper in my skin. Surely all the grit was out now, right? I guess not, because then came a soothing period in front of a steamer (with soft music playing), and I was *steam cleaned.* Then came the manual cleansing of certain areas to remove congested buildup. At long last, the pores were finally clear. I guess I shouldn't have been surprised it took so long to get my fifty-year-old face finally cleaned!

Before going to a spa, you don't focus on getting your makeup and hairstyle perfect. Instead, you throw on casual clothes and go as you are, assuming the experts will work on you and turn you out nicely. "Come as you are," Jesus also says to all people today. "Come with all your insecurity, your fears, your depression, your imperfections. Come and I will love you into wholeness. I will heal you and give you hope."

And we come, but we sure drag a lot in the door with us, don't we? In his little book *Give It All to Him: A Story of New Beginnings,* Max Lucado tells a parable of people dragging huge garbage bags, full of shame, sin, and past regrets to the city dump and then throwing them on top of a man who crumbles under the weight and takes their garbage on himself so they can live unencumbered. This man is the Christ figure, and, yes, he does emerge from the garbage dump, signaling resurrection; and that all who have trusted in Him can have new life.

We have all been, figuratively speaking, dirtied by wrong choices and unhealthy living. We can put on hair color, makeup, and a whole new wardrobe. We can douse ourselves in expensive perfume. But those are only another layer—maybe a beautiful one—covering the dirt. However, we still smell. Dirty hair may be a nice color and style, but it itches when it's not clean.

If we truly examine our inner lives today, we may find we, too, are covered in grime, shame, guilt, depression, and sin—which is, by the way, any time we choose to go our way and not God's way. We may think we're clean, but just as I discovered during my facial, what we need is deep cleansing.

And Christ is the One to do this. "He saved us—not by works of righteousness that we had done, but according to His mercy, through the washing of regeneration and renewal by the Holy Spirit. This [Spirit] He poured out on us abundantly through Jesus Christ our Savior, so that having been justified by His grace, we may become heirs with the hope of eternal life" (Titus 3:5–7). Once again, here is that reference to washing as part of His mercy. This is certainly one of the first elements in any spa for our souls.

Cleansing not only makes us clean but it *restores* us just as scrubbing away old skin cells helps bring life to new ones. And everyone needs restoration for we have all become dirtied and soiled by the buildup over time of layer after layer of wrong choices and lazy living. What does it take for us to finally reach the point King David did when he lamented in Psalm 51:10, "God, create a clean heart for me and renew a steadfast spirit within me."

We begin by recognizing that we need deep cleansing. When I went for my facial, I thought I was scrubbed and ready to go. I was wrong. Sometimes it takes another person to point out areas that need to be addressed. And if you have a friend or family member willing to do this, thank God. Even King David needed help to face reality in his life.

You remember the infamous story in 2 Samuel 11 of the king who one day saw a beautiful woman bathing on her rooftop. He decided then and there he simply must have her for himself. It didn't matter that Bathsheba was married to Uriah, one of David's trusted warriors. He wanted her, and he took her to his bed. After all, he was the king! But when she became pregnant, he realized he'd better make sure her soldier husband came home from the front for a conjugal visit. Unfortunately, Uriah refused to lie with his wife in deference to his duty. So David contrived a plot for Uriah to be killed in battle. With the husband out of the way, David married Bathsheba. "She became his wife and bore him a son. However, the LORD considered what David had done to be evil" (2 Sam. 11:27b).

He was soiled, wasn't he? His hands were dirty from sexual sin and murder. It took the prophet Nathan to help him see his need for confession and forgiveness. Nathan told his king a story about a rich man who had a lot of sheep and cattle and a poor man who had only one little lamb he loved like part of his family. But when the rich man wanted to feed a guest, he didn't take one of his own for the meal but instead took the poor man's lamb and made lamb stew. On hearing this, David was enraged and shouted to Nathan that the rich man had done wrong and deserved to die.

But Nathan merely responded by looking his king in the eye and saying, "You are the man!" The prophet went on to give God's warning: "'I anointed you king over Israel, and I delivered you from the hand of Saul. I gave your master's house to you and your master's wives into your arms, and I gave you the house of Israel and Judah, and if that was not enough, I would have given you even more. Why then have you despised the command of the LORD by doing what I consider evil? You struck down Uriah the Hittite with the sword and took his wife as your own wife—you murdered him with the Ammonite's sword. Now therefore, the sword will never leave your house because you despised Me and took the wife of Uriah the Hittite to be your own wife'" (2 Sam. 12:7–10).

As reality stared him in the face, David admitted his sin against the Lord (2 Sam. 12:13), and Nathan assured him that while David himself would not die, his newborn son's life would be forfeited. What a terrible consequence of his own sin! David fasted and prayed, and yet the baby did die. Then the king and father *washed* and went to the Lord and worshiped Him. I suspect he was never the same again.

I am so grateful this story is in the Bible because I, too, have sinned and had a wake-up call when I needed to come before God, begging for mercy and cleansing. Psalm 51 is the most beautiful record of David's entreaty to a loving God: "Be gracious to me, God, according to Your faithful love; according to Your abundant compassion, blot out my rebellion. Wash away my guilt, and cleanse me from my sin. For I am conscious of my rebellion, and my sin is always before me. Against You—You alone—I have sinned and done this evil in Your sight. So You are right when You pass sentence; You are blameless when You judge. Indeed, I was guilty [when I] was born; I was sinful when my mother conceived me. Surely You desire integrity in the inner self, and You teach me wisdom deep within. Purify me with hyssop, and I will be clean; wash me, and I will be whiter than snow" (vv. 1–7).

David knew his only hope was if God would cleanse him from within. Just an outer scrubbing wouldn't do—his sin required deep cleansing. And David was ready to submit to whatever God chose. He also had the faith that God not only had the power to cleanse him but the desire to do so as well. God loves us so much that He wants us to be restored to Him and restored to full emotional and spiritual health. He wants us to live pure lives not because He's a tyrant desiring to quash all our fun, but because He knows that's the only way for us to experience all He has for us in this life. Our former lives lead us only into bondage. "You will know the truth, and the truth will set you free" (John 8:32).

Exfoliate. Great word, isn't it? And it means to roughly remove the old skin in order to release a fresh layer of new skin. Perhaps God needs to perform an exfoliation on us. But facing the sin in our lives is hard, nearly impossible without the help of a loving Father, One who requires only that we come to Him just as we are and kneel before Him in contrition and confession. As David knew, "The sacrifice pleasing to God is a broken spirit. God, You will not despise a broken and humbled heart," (Ps. 51:17). Think of godly people you know today. Chances are they, too, have had experiences in which they were broken before their heavenly Father and discovered God's mercy and grace at their lowest point. A rough scrub hurts for a time, but it's good for us.

Hymnist Fanny Crosby knew that God's deep cleansing not only changes us from within but also empowers us through the Holy Spirit to live differently—a difference that should be evidenced from without. "Faith in Jesus" is one of the eight thousand hymns she wrote during her ninety-five years:

Gracious Lord, Thou canst make me clean;
Lord, I am pleading still;
Now I hear from Thy lips divine,

"Child, thou hast faith—I will";
Joy to my soul, great joy has come,
Mourning and tears are o'er;
Sweet are Thy words of love to me,
"Go thou, and sin no more."

But even as we try to *go and sin no more,* most of us find an unexpected "souvenir" from our experiences—shame. Oh, the world might not see it at first glance. When I first met Cynthia Spell, who is now a sister of my heart, I was greatly impressed by both her brains and beauty. Not only did I learn she had been a therapist with the Minirth-Meier Clinic for seven years and was a wife and young mother of three children, but she also had published an excellent book: *Deceived by Shame, Desired by God.* However, the connection that seemed to make us immediate kindred spirits was our mutual experiences of God's grace and mercy reaching into our lives and delivering us from perfectionism and living for the approval of others.

Cynthia observed that the souvenir of shame can cause women to seek to fill the hurting places in their hearts with everything but God—relationships, food, possessions, control, alcohol, drugs, sex, power, shopping, exercise, and activities. "Through my own recovery journey and the experience of counseling many shame-filled women, I have become convinced that most of the shaming sin we get into is based on our own emotional neediness. We each desperately long to feel valuable, important, cared for, listened to, esteemed, loved, and completely accepted for who we are. We seek both to accomplish something worthwhile with our lives and to win the approval of others. . . . Until we clearly understand who God truly is, how passionately He loves us, and how deeply He desires to restore us into right relationship with Him, we will continue to search for fulfillment in unsafe places."[1]

I'm reminded of Pigpen in the *Peanuts* gang. He's the little guy who's always dirty. Wherever he goes, a dust cloud follows, and it appears he has been dirty for so long that no bath or expensive spa treatment could clean him. "Shame feels a lot like Pigpen looks. Often, the cloud that always hovers near includes fear, anxiety, loneliness, guilt over past sin, depression, sadness, a bitter spirit towards those who damaged you, the shame of addiction, a painful divorce, and rejection. Pigpen seems isolated from others at times. No one wants to eat the simple dirty lemon drops, which are the only thing he has to offer."[2]

Have you ever felt like that—dirty and rejected? Do you know that God, the Creator and Sustainer of the universe, loves you so much that He wants to restore you to Himself? He did it for the people of Israel after their many times of going astray, and He will do it for us too. "Whoever remains in Zion and whoever is left in Jerusalem will be called holy—all in Jerusalem who are destined to live—when the Lord has washed away the filth of the daughters of Zion and cleansed the bloodguilt from the heart of Jerusalem by a spirit of judgment and a spirit of burning" (Isa. 4:3–4).

God is the One who does the cleansing. My friend Jennifer Kennedy Dean uses this word picture to help us understand the process. "Visualize a clear glass. Do you see it? Now imagine that glass filled with dirty, nasty water. Look closely and see the dirt particles floating in the water. See how cloudy it is? A layer of scum glazes the top and sediment has settled on the bottom.

"Now pour the water out of the glass. When the dirty water is gone, what remains? Is the glass clean? No, the dirt clings to the sides. The sediment may be rearranged, but it's still there. What will happen when you put the clean water into the glass? The water will pick up the dirt on the glass and the clean water will be contaminated.

"Let that picture represent for you the effect of self-effort to produce purity in yourself. No matter how hard you try, you cannot make yourself pure.

"Revisualize your glass full of dirty water. This time, put the glass under a faucet and turn on the water. Now watch what happens. The continual flow of fresh, clean water begins to push out the old dirty water. Eventually, the force of the flow even disturbs the sediment on the bottom and washes it out. Finally, the glass is clean — it's filled with clean water, and clean water is spilling over the edges.

"What's the secret? The fresh and continual flow of water." [3]

> *Gracious Lord, Thou*
> *canst make me clean;*
> *Lord, I am pleading still;*
> *Now I hear from*
> *Thy lips divine,*
> *"Child, thou hast*
> *faith—I will."*
>
> —FANNY CROSBY, "FAITH IN JESUS"

Yes, being cleansed by Living Water is only the beginning. But it can lead to great things as we seek daily to grow in Christ likeness, because we are called to share in His glory. I don't understand why and how God would choose someone like me to bear His glory. But then, why did he call an adulterer, King David, a man after His own heart? I believe it was because David finally recognized that the way he was living was not God's way, and he then sought cleansing and restoration.

"Do you not know that the unjust will not inherit God's kingdom? Do not be deceived: no sexually immoral people, idolaters, adulterers, male prostitutes, homosexuals, thieves, greedy people, drunkards, revilers, or swindlers will inherit God's kingdom. Some of you were like this; but you were washed, you were sanctified, you were justified in the name of the Lord Jesus Christ and by the Spirit of our God" (1 Cor. 6:9–11).

When God wants to show His glory, He causes ordinary people to be and do what they could never be and do without His power. So the result is that others recognize it is God in them, and not their own resources achieving such things. This, in turn, glorifies God. We all can live like that and glorify Him through transformed lives.

God's promise is to restore the broken. "Restore the joy of Your salvation to me, and give me a willing spirit" (Ps. 51:12). Then we shine for Him in a way only dreamed of before. When my parents downsized recently, they gave my sisters and me some of their things so we could now enjoy them with our own families. I received the coffee and tea silver service and several other silver serving dishes just in time for Easter dinner. But, of course, when they arrived, they were severely tarnished from months of storage. In fact, they were so black my daughter couldn't understand my excitement at owning these family treasures.

So I set about to clean them. I purchased several kinds of silver polish, rubber gloves, and polishing cloths. It took all morning, lots of elbow grease, and hard scrubbing, but it was worth it. When Maggie came home from school that afternoon, she was amazed at the shiny silver all over the dining room table. "Why, it's like a mirror, Mama. You can actually see yourself in this tray!" she exclaimed.

And she was right. The true beauty had been hidden by neglect and tarnish. It took attention and commitment, but the results were amazing. Not only that, but I was now energized and inspired and promptly proceeded to attack my souvenir spoon collection (more than one hundred silver spoons from around the world) with the silver polish. Hey, I was on a roll!

That's what cleansing does for our spirits too. We become energized to shine for Christ with the new glory now reflected in us. "We all, with unveiled faces, are reflecting the glory of the Lord and are being transformed into the same image from glory to glory; this is from the Lord who is the Spirit" (2 Cor. 3:18).

Do you know God's plan for furthering Christ's kingdom here on earth? You and I—His people. We are plan A. And there is no plan B! He cleanses us through rebirth and then gives us His grace when we blow it and repent. Finally, He promises we will share in His glory, to shine for Him. So let's get started!

Spiritual Personal Assessment

Scripture. Read Psalm 51 in your own Bible, and underline phrases of King David's with which you can identify. Make this your own prayer.

Journal. In your private journal recall a time when you chose to go your way instead of God's way (a specific time of sin). Write what you did, how you felt, and the consequences of that sin. Then go before God in prayer, confessing your sin and be restored to Him.

Discussion. After David and Bathsheba's first baby died as a consequence of sin, David washed himself and worshiped the Lord. What do you think was in his mind at that time?

Do you remember that their next baby was Solomon who later became the wisest king over Israel? What does this reveal to you about God's character?

Spa Treatment. Give yourself a facial. Inexpensive masks and cleansing scrubs can be purchased at any pharmacy. Be sure to clean thoroughly, and then apply the mask cream to the chin before working your way over your cheeks and up to your forehead. Then apply it from the upper part of your nose to just below your eyes and finally to the bridge of your nose. Leave the mask on for ten to twenty minutes while you relax. Cleanse your face with warm water, pat dry, and then apply toner and moisturizer. Don't you feel better already?

CHAPTER 3

The Master's Massage

"As the Father has loved me, I have also loved you.
Remain in My love. If you keep My commands you
will remain in My love, just as I have kept
My Father's commands and remain in His love. . . .
This is My command: love one another as I have
loved you. No one has greater love than this."

—JOHN 15:9–10, 12–13A

I think I was purring. At least, it was a quiet moan, barely audible above the calming sounds of the seagulls and ocean waves. I knew I was in heaven, even if for only fifty minutes. I was experiencing the ultimate of luxury—a massage at the Sea Island Spa.

The weekend before, I had spoken at a large conference nearby on the Georgia coast, and I was delighted that my mother, sister, and aunt were able to join me for the event. But we didn't want it to end, so Mama had graciously treated us to an overnight at the Cloister—a girlfriends gathering full of laughter and shared memories. It didn't take much for me to talk myself into scheduling an early Monday morning massage before catching my plane. "After all," I reasoned, "when else will I have the chance to experience one of the top five spas in the country?" I was here and I was going for it!

When I arrived at the women's locker room, an assistant gave me a robe and spa sandals and guided me into several different treatment centers. I started off in the sauna, surrounded by hot stones that did their job of making me sweat profusely. Then I was placed in the steam room, where I was literally steam cleaned. Fortunately, all these were timed, so I was not overdone. Then a nice shower and voilà! I was already feeling like a new woman. The assistant guided me up to a beautifully appointed room with hot tea, fresh fruit, a comfortable lounge chair overlooking the Atlantic Ocean, and copies of reading material. I sat there awhile, thanking God for what He had done at the conference as well as for this precious time with my family. Then I was summoned to a private room and met my massage therapist.

She was a master. For the next fifty minutes I was transported from the cares of this world to utter relaxation and repose. The quiet music set the tone. My aching muscles received pressure, then kneading, stretching, and rest, all lubricated with scented lavender oil. By the time the therapist finished, I felt like jelly. Yes, I did purr like a kitten.

The by-products of massage are many—increased blood and lymph circulation, eased tension, and energetic revitalization. Even while I was experiencing all those at the spa, I wondered how I could take this experience with me to my everyday, busy life back home in Connecticut.

Then it hit me. Sometimes God's love is like a massage, constantly stroking me and enveloping me in its intimacy and care. If I live each day with the awareness of being His beloved, I also can learn how to relax and receive all He gives me. But massage can have both a stimulating effect as well as a calming effect. Sometimes the kneading hurts sore muscles as it does the necessary work of loosening the tension! The Master's massage is not physical but spiritual, yet it certainly has physical benefits. When I am convinced of the unconditional love of God, I can live free of worry and fear. I can submit to Him my schedule and ask Him to guide me when to say yes and when to say no. When I am defined by the fact that I am God's beloved, I have the self-esteem that enables me to withstand ridicule or rejection from others. And even when I'm most alone, God's presence envelopes me with love and comfort.

Why don't we experience the Master's massage of love more? I believe we view God's love the same way we have experienced human love throughout our lives. All of us have been disappointed in love, felt hurt, or been deserted. Someone who promised to love us always, someone with whom we shared our most intimate of selves, that person let us down or deliberately deceived us. We felt burned, and we vowed we would never get close again. It would simply be too hard to face that kind of thwarted love. So we built a little wall around our heart, for protection, of course. And now we are wary of love.

The problem with this, of course, is that God's love is *nothing* like the love we give and the love we receive from fellow sinners. God's love is *truly unconditional.* The Hebrew term for this in the Old Testament is *chesed,* which we translate into "loving-kindness" or "unfailing love." But even those words cannot fully convey what God means by *chesed.* He means forever. For always. With no strings attached. He means that He loves us not for anything we have done or have not done, not for how we look or act or how faithful or unfaithful we have been on our spiritual journeys. God's love is there for each of us simply because we are His children.

I was in my late thirties when I first gave birth to a baby girl. She was actually my fourth child, as I had adopted my first three children when they were ages four, seven, and nine. So Maggie was my first baby. Do you remember your first baby? You loved her immediately. And it wasn't because she was beautiful or brilliant, though mine surely was. You loved her immediately because she was yours! That's how God feels about us, His children. And all of us who have given our hearts and lives to Jesus are certainly called children of God.

He is our heavenly Father, a loving parent. But yet again, here I stray. For I am once again trying to understand God's divine love in my own limited human terms. Yes, He is our heavenly Father and, yes, He does love us the way we love our babies. But that still doesn't embrace the depth or totality of His love. We simply cannot comprehend it. Because we know that as parents we fail. Some have had miserable examples of fathers and mothers, and some have been miserable examples of fathers and mothers. And yet, God longs to embrace us like a father, to cover us like a mother.

In Jeremiah 31:3b the Lord tells his people, "I have loved you with an everlasting love; therefore, I have continued to extend faithful love to you." He has been pursuing us and seeking to draw us closer to Himself because He wants us near Him. God loves us because His very nature is love, and He also loves us because He made us.

Massage therapy is very intimate. I mean, you have to take off all your clothes! Talk about feeling vulnerable. And so it is with the kind of relationship we have with God. Because He made us in His image, we have the potential for an intimate relationship with Him. But we don't have to be nervous or shy as we stand naked before Him. Remember, He is the One who created us and knows us inside out already. Did you know there is nothing you can do to make God love you more and nothing you can do to make Him love you less? In human terms perhaps we can best understand His love in this way: God loves you so much that if He had a refrigerator, your picture would be on it! We are that precious to Him.

I lived for many years thinking I had to be perfect to make God love me more so I tried desperately to be perfect. I thought if I *did* and *said* and *read* and *professed* everything *right,* I would be loved by God. But I blew it—lots of times. And I'll bet you've blown it too. When we fail in relationships, we often find ourselves rejected and tossed aside, which makes us try even harder to be perfect, thus repeating a never-ending cycle. It took me a long time to realize that God loves me not because I'm perfect but because I'm *His.* While it's true we don't have to earn God's love by being perfect, the most amazing thing is that when we know His love, our greatest desire becomes pleasing Him.

Paula Rinehart, author of *Perfect Every Time,* shared her own struggles in this area. "Whatever I said I knew was true about God, what I really believed was that my effort could wrest from Him a love and acceptance based on my performance. I could not receive grace until I stepped off the treadmill and waited with empty, needy hands. Until I disconnected my longing to be loved from my efforts to please."[1]

The hymnist F. M. Lehman penned these words in 1917, and they still assure me of the unfathomable nature of God's love.

The love of God is greater far than tongue or pen can ever tell;
It goes beyond the highest star, and reaches to the lowest hell;
O love of God, how rich and pure! How measureless and strong!
It shall forevermore endure the saints' and angel's song.
Could we with ink the oceans fill, and were the skies of parchment made,
Were every stalk on earth a quill, and every man a scribe by trade,
To write the love of God above would drain the ocean dry,
Nor could the scroll contain the whole, though stretched from sky to sky.

That means that wherever you and I are today—physically, emotionally, spiritually, financially, geographically—we are never beyond the unfailing love of God.

This tenacious love of God is both eternal and changeless. "The steadfast love of the Lord is from everlasting to everlasting" (Ps. 103:17a RSV). God decided to love me even before I existed! Before I was even born He already knew the worst about me, and nothing I do now surprises or disillusions Him. As James I. Packer wrote in *Knowing God,* "God's love to me is utterly realistic, based at every point on the prior knowledge of the worst about me, so that no discovery now can disillusion Him about me in the way I am so often disillusioned about myself, and quench His determination to bless me."[2]

God has made a permanent choice to love us. That's real security! All of us have turned from God's love at one time or another. The book of Hosea is a wonderful story of God declaring that He still loves His people in the middle of their rebellion. "How can I give you up, Israel? . . . My heart will not let me do it! My love for you is too strong" (Hos. 11:8 GNB). Have you turned away from God's love? Do not be discouraged. Do not give up on Him, for He certainly has never given up on you.

> *God touches us with His love and we are never the same again!*

I recently ran across a copy of an old Christmas Card. I've always designed my own cards and included insight from that year's experiences. That particular year I had just turned thirty, completed an eventful ministry/ speaking trip through Africa and was about to make one of the most important decisions of my life. No wonder this is the verse I shared: "Yet I am always with you; you hold me by my right hand. You guide me with your counsel, and afterward you will take me into glory. Whom have I in heaven but you? And earth has nothing I desire besides you. My flesh and my heart may fail, but God is the strength of my heart and my portion forever" (Ps. 73:23–26 NIV).

Yes, one day our bodies and even our souls may grow weak and waste away, as the psalmist says. Or worse, we may inwardly and outwardly fail to trust and obey the Lord. But we can always return to Him and receive His *chesed*, everlasting love.

Counselor Brenda Waggoner once described a life-changing experience of God's love "like a balm of concentrated forgiveness being massaged directly into my heart, I began to feel comforted, held, blessed." As she pictured Him, she was startled to realize He was smiling at her, not scowling with judgment. "He gazed into my eyes with tenderness and compassion such as I'd never seen or felt. . . . After a few minutes thoughts began to come: *Jesus loves me.* Reaching for a spiral notebook and pen, I wrote down: Jesus loves me. The reality of the words on the page began to sink into my heart, as I gratefully returned His gaze."

Brenda wrote a prayer of praise to the God showering her with love and acceptance:

I was a lonely little girl . . . and Jesus loved me.
I tried to make my first marriage work, but I didn't know how
. . . and Jesus loved me.
My children suffered pain and loss due, in part, to my actions
. . . and Jesus loved me.
I got angry at God because I didn't get the answers I wanted
. . . and Jesus loved me.
I threw up my hands and admitted failure . . . and Jesus loved me.
There is hope for my future . . . because Jesus loved me.[3]

The word *massage* comes from the Greek root *masso,* which means "to touch." God touches us with His love, and we are never the same again. One reason massage therapy is so popular today is because it has many benefits. It improves blood circulation, prevents and treats muscle pain and spasm, reduces tension and anxiety, calms the nervous system, and promotes a sense of relaxation and well-being. What's not to like? But if massage can do all that, the Master's massage can do so much more!

How would you live differently if you truly believed God's incredible love for you? King David couldn't help but tell others of this great love he had experienced. "I will sing about the LORD's faithful love forever; with my mouth I will proclaim Your faithfulness to all generations" (Ps. 89:1).

I had an epiphany of sorts once while sitting in a parked car with my then fifteen-year-old daughter, Maggie. Waiting for her brother, we started singing as we often do when we are together. Usually it's golden oldies or praise songs, but that day we started on old ballads from the 1950s, ones my parents had enjoyed and I had passed on to Maggie.

As I was crooning, my teenager interrupted me. "Every time you sing, Mama, it's like you are telling me a story." Then she did a perfect imitation of my singing, and it *did* sound as if I was telling a story. True, when she was a baby, I had always put her to sleep with my own version of Sinatra—"When your mama loves you, it's no good unless she loves you all the way"—along with the lullaby from *The Music Man*: "Goodnight, my Maggie, goodnight my love. Sleep tight, my Maggie, sleep tight my love." During the junior high years, I often sang Charlie Chaplin's ballad, "Smile, though your heart is breaking, smile, even though it's aching . . ." After all, isn't that what makes good love songs—personalizing them for your own situation?

In a way I *was* telling her a story, the story of my love for her so she would feel secure and go to sleep. And, in the middle of adolescence, she reminded me that it worked! Of course, I also spent a lot of time also telling actual stories to all my four children, passing on the oral tradition of our family and of God's faithfulness.

Do you sing or tell stories to your children and grandchildren? Do they know how much they are loved and treasured? Are your presence and your peace a source of security to them in an increasingly insecure world?

Most importantly, have you shared the greatest story ever told? You know, the one in which the Creator greatly loves His creation, but His people turn from Him and go their own way and He tries to win them back through prophets, pestilence, and perilous journeys, but they still rebel. So the only way He can finally get their attention is to take the biggest risk of all—to become like one of them. He gives up everything to join their humanity and to show them love and a better way, culminating in a final dramatic proof of love by suffering the punishment they deserved through His death on a cross and then miraculously coming back to remind them that all who follow Him will live forever!

Talk about an incredible love story!

And the best part is that this can easily be personalized for any loved one. "For God so loved *Maggie* that he gave his one and only Son, that if *Maggie* believes in Him *Maggie* shall not perish but *Maggie* shall have eternal life" (John 3:16 NIV).

Are you living today in the middle of a grand story? Or are you settling for whatever small story you can wrap up in while coasting the rest of your days? God has called each of His children to play a part in what He is doing in the world today. I'm so passionate about encouraging others to live fully the Life Story that God is authoring that I wrote a whole book about it — *Role of a Lifetime — Your Part in God's Story*. No matter what your age or stage in life, you can write a new story and pass it on to those you love. Your vibrancy and beliefs will come through whether you are singing, working, volunteering, or even baby-sitting. And others may just pick up the love story too.

So, don't go any further in your "spa" treatment until you have embraced the Master's massage and settled into the love He longs to give you. Give Him your heart and live each day through faith, receiving His grace and peace for all time and into eternity.

Spiritual Personal Assessment

Scripture. Turn to Psalm 136, which is a litany of praise for God's never-ending love. Read it aloud to yourself, letting the repeated phrase "His love is eternal" sink into your soul. Add a few praises of your own, for example "Give thanks to the heavenly Father—His love is eternal. Who daily protects my children, Justin, Tim, Fiona, and Maggie—His love is eternal."

Journal. List the characteristics of love found in 1 Corinthians 13, noting how you have experienced God's love in that way. Also, write down your own evaluation of how your love measures up to that characteristic. Write a prayer for seeking this more excellent way.

Discussion. Can you recall a time when you experienced the Master's massage and knew in your heart that you were deeply loved and totally accepted? How do you respond to such love?

What surprises you most about God's love? Do you ever find yourself trying to do more in order to earn His love? Is there anything hindering you from accepting His gift of grace—not based on performance but simply because you are His daughter?

Spa Treatment. Give yourself a head massage! This is ideal for getting rid of headaches brought on by stress, noise, fluorescent lights, and long periods seated at the computer screen. Wash your face first and remember to breathe deeply and slowly through your mouth as you massage.

1. Place your middle fingers parallel to your eyes and just above your cheekbones. Using firm but gentle circular motions, massage for one minute.

2. Move your thumbs along the underside of your eyebrows—along the bone at the top of your eye socket. Feel where this bone meets the bridge of your nose and close your eyes. Feel

for a point where there is a small indentation and with very gentle pressure press your thumbs into the points. Hold for ten seconds; release and repeat three times.

3. Move the middle fingers of your hands to the back of your head and feel at the base of your skull for the point where the top of your neck meets your skull. Using gentle circular movements, massage this area with your fingertips for one minute.

4. Now place the palms of your hands on the top of your skull and gently massage your scalp for one minute. When you've finished take a few deep breaths. Lift your shoulders toward your ears, hold them there for five to ten seconds, and then let them drop back down in their natural position. By doing this a couple of times, your neck will feel lengthened and your head less weighty.

CHAPTER 4

Body Image

~ ❧ ~

*Do you not know that your body is a sanctuary
of the Holy Spirit who is in you, whom you have from God?
You are not your own, for you were bought at a price;
therefore glorify God in your body.*

—1 CORINTHIANS 6:19–20

When I was a little girl I spent a lot of time with a naked woman—my Barbie doll. Yes, I grew up in the early 1960s when playing with Barbie, Ken, Midge, and Skipper was all the rage. My friends and I would gather for hours to arrange houses, picnics, and beach scenes. But mostly, we dressed and undressed those Barbie dolls. We collected all her designer clothing and lots of bathing suits and accessories. I still have two trunks full of my Barbies and all their paraphernalia. They're probably worth a lot of money, so let me know if you want to take them off my hands.

I guess in many ways Barbie was my first introduction to glamour and fashion and what a grown-up gal should look like! And yet, like many other baby boomers, I'm paying the price to this day for allowing her to shape my views on body image. For compared to Barbie, *none* of us measures up to this ideal. And how in the world could we?

If a Barbie doll were a real person, she would be seven feet two with a forty-inch bust, a twenty-two-inch waist, and thirty-six-inch hips. Her neck is twice the length of a normal human's neck. An average woman is five feet four with a thirty-seven-inch bust, a twenty-nine-inch waist, and forty-inch hips. She wears a size 12. In fact, 60 percent of American women wear a size 12 or larger! So there aren't that many real-life Barbies walking around today. *Marie Claire* magazine revealed these facts in addition to the announcement, "There are 3 billion women who DON'T look like supermodels and only 8 who DO!"

Let's face it, girlfriend, the media is doing a number on us all. We are bombarded by images of thin, airbrushed women on billboards and television, in movies and magazines, and through every kind of advertisement possible: *If* you purchase this product, you *will* look like this model! Only the model doesn't even really look like that—her image has usually been digitally altered and airbrushed to her best advantage. Yet one scientific study that used eight popular magazines documented that a woman's body satisfaction was greatly influenced by her exposure to the thin ideal presented in those fashion magazines.

Another study revealed that 69 percent of *Playboy* models and 69 percent of Miss America contestants weighed 15 percent or more *below* the expected weight for their age and height category. This is downright unhealthy; in fact, being 15 percent below one's expected weight is one criterion for anorexia. This standard of being thin, perfectly proportioned with beautiful hair, glowing skin, fabulous makeup, and the best clothes money can buy is dangerous. It leaves most of us feeling inadequate and dissatisfied with our bodies. We need to revisit our whole view of body image—physical appearance, size, and shape.

Marcia Hutchinson, author of *Transforming Body Image,* stated, "Our body image is formed out of every experience we have ever had—parents, role models, and peers who give us an idea of what it is like to love and value a body. Image is formed from the positive and the negative feedback from people whose opinions matter to us. It is also the way we ourselves have perceived our body to fit or not fit the cultural image."[1]

Due to all these factors, most of us look in the mirror and fashion a distorted perception of our bodies. Because we don't look like those glamorous media images, we view ourselves as totally lacking. In a *Glamour* magazine survey, 75 percent of women ages eighteen to thirty-five believed they were fat, but only 25 percent were actually medically overweight. Forty-five percent of underweight women said that they were too fat. Yes, obesity is a big problem in our country today (pun intended), but not everyone who thinks she's obese really is.

In Dr. Deborah Newman's excellent book *Comfortable in Your Own Skin – Making Peace with Your Body Image,* she said, "A healthy body image is characterized by three major components: respect, care and perspective." Do you *respect* your body as a miraculous testimony of God your Creator? With King David, do you praise God "because I have been remarkably and wonderfully made" (Ps. 139:14a)? Do you take *care* of your body through proper nutrition, exercise, and rest? "And do not offer any parts of [body] to sin as weapons for unrighteousness" (Rom. 6:13a). And, finally, do you maintain a healthy *perspective* about your body by not comparing yourself to others? "For we don't dare classify or compare ourselves with some who commend themselves. But in measuring themselves by themselves and comparing themselves to themselves, they lack understanding" (2 Cor. 10:12).[2]

One of my friends shared her continual struggle with body image perspective. "Recently I have been hearing the voice of God calling me to reevaluate the way I view my body. I picked up countless messages from the culture and from my family that being thin is good and beautiful and healthy. I hear God telling me it's finally time to break the tyranny of those messages. But even more profoundly, I hear God calling me to shake off our culture's values and live my life for an audience of one: God himself."[3]

I've learned a lot about acceptance and being created in God's image from my eldest son, Justin. Born with intellectual disabilities, this young man has never let his limitations get him down. In fact, he is one of the most self-confident people I know, because he truly believes he was made in God's image. Whenever I praise him with words such as "Justin, I enjoy being with you. You're good company," he responds simply, "I know."

So, because Justin is an athlete, our family has been involved with Special Olympics International for more than twenty-five years. We can't praise this organization enough for how it encourages those with differing abilities. Before each sports event, the athletes repeat the Special Olympics pledge: "Let me win. But if I cannot win, let me be brave in the attempt." That's not a bad theme for all of us as we seek to dispel messages of those who put us down or who have contributed negatively to how we currently view our bodies.

It has been a lifelong journey for me to finally fully embrace what God says about me and my body instead of heeding all those other messages. Throughout that journey, I have experienced life as a chubby child, a slender teen, and then a morbidly obese adult. At some point in my life, after too much yo-yo dieting and too many weight fluctuations, I finally gave up trying to lose weight and began to turn to food to meet my emotional needs. I remained in that rut for many years. I was miserable, and my preoccupation with my weight affected every area of my life: physical/medical, emotional, and spiritual. My sin was not being overweight; my sin was turning to another substance (food) to meet needs that only God can meet.

It would be an understatement to say I was not being a good steward of the health He had entrusted to me. Over time, food had become much more than sustenance—food was comfort, love, security, companionship, distraction, and a way to numb myself so I wouldn't have to face the real issues that needed spiritual transformation.

Suffice it to say there was a day several years ago when I cried out to God, "I don't want to live like this anymore! Whatever it takes, I am willing to do the hard work of change. Show me. Guide me. Be with me."

And He did. And I did. And the whys and wherefores are not as important as you might think. There is no magic bullet; everything you have heard is true. Eat healthy. Exercise regularly. But, of course, the process is always more complicated than that, and I had a team of medical personnel, nutritionists, and prayer warriors without whom I never could have reached this point. Each of us is unique—our bodies, metabolism, ages, personalities and psyches, genetic predispositions, and lifetime habits.

But wherever we are physically and spiritually there comes a time when most of us need to say, "I don't want to live like this anymore." And that's when we are most receptive to the extreme makeover—the ultimate metamorphosis of a transformed life.

> *You have to change the way you see before you can change the way you look.*
> —Nick Yphantides

I now weigh myself every Monday morning (even when I don't want to) and record it in my journal. I am now truly average—average height, average weight, wearing average sizes. It is amazing how much *less* emphasis I place on body image now that I'm more fit.

And yet I *never forget*. Each day I must make healthy choices regarding what I eat and how much I move around. I cannot afford to go back to lazy and unhealthy habits. I have paid too high a cost to get to this place.

Mostly for me it is a matter of perspective. I always wanted food to be just food, to take its place of importance, but not greater. When I realized I was scheduling my life around food (instead of food around my life), I knew I was in trouble. I am gradually participating in the process of restoring my soul through turning to God for deep peace and satisfaction. Truly, "he restores my soul" (Ps. 23:3a NIV).

"The world offers you peace if you look a certain way. Does that peace ever come? Are Hollywood filmmakers, advertisers, and the fashion industry centered on a meaningful relationship with God when they feed us beliefs about what it means to be beautiful? True beauty is experienced as you bask in the center of God's love and care for you—all of you—spirit, body, and soul."[4]

People go to spas for many reasons, but one of them is that they are ready for some kind of change. Are you ready for a change in your body? And I'm not talking about plastic surgery! There are always actions that can help usher us into greater physical health, but many of these also have terrific benefits for our spiritual health as well. The body and soul are very much intertwined.

Virtually every health expert agrees that the path to true wellness lies not in the latest diet craze but in a permanent lifestyle change. One of my heroes is Carole Lewis, who in 1981 became involved with (and later the Director of) First Place 4 Health, a ministry which encourages balance in four areas of health: physical, mental, emotional and spiritual — see www.FirstPlace4Health.com. She has helped countless believers experience victory in weight loss and other dramatic changes in their health. After being involved with FP4H for a number of years I totally agree with Carole's premise that "The only way that people are going to lose weight and keep it off is with a lifestyle change. It's not dieting."

When my husband had heart surgery almost fifteen years ago, we finally began to take nutrition seriously. I discovered what most healthy people already know—natural foods serve the human body better than manufactured foods. Now this is distressing news for someone like me who likes "quick fixes." But it certainly is possible to eat healthy even if you are somewhat culinary- impaired. "Lean meats, including poultry and beef, balanced with generous portions of fruits and vegetables, and sprinkled with nuts and whole grains; provide the best fuel for the body. Conversely, processed foods, bleached wheat, chemical sweeteners, and other packaged products quickly convert to fat and threaten our well being."[5]

Although my goal in this book is not to direct specific ways to lose weight, I offer a few observations about food. From the time we are born we equate food with getting our needs met, so it's only natural to equate food with feeling better. To complicate that, food is not something we can give up totally; we have to eat to live. So the question becomes "How can I eat in a healthy way, both for my body (physical nourishment) and my soul (keeping food in proper perspective)?"

Dr. Deborah Newman offers the following suggestions to establish healthy eating patterns:

- Schedule three meals a day at regular times.

- Try to eat with your family at the table as often as possible.

- Don't nibble during meal preparation.

- When you eat, concentrate on experiencing your food, its texture, smell, and taste, and avoid shoveling everything into your mouth.

- Eat slowly. Put your fork down between bites.

- Drink half your body weight in ounces of fresh water daily. For example, if you weigh 120 pounds, you should drink sixty ounces of water each day.

- Enjoy pleasant music and conversation during your meals.

- Recognize it's normal to feel full after a meal, and your belt or waistband will feel a little tighter. Don't condemn yourself for eating and enjoying your meal.

- Don't keep a record of forbidden foods. You should include desserts and foods you like (in proper proportion) in your regular eating schedule.

- Don't eat in the car, bus, bedroom, or bathroom, or on the run.

- Don't try to lose weight too fast. Losing one-half pound a week is healthier for your body.

- Eat fewer fatty foods and simple sugars.

- Eat more fresh fruits, vegetables, and whole grains.

- Engage in moderate physical activity.[6]

Exercising also is important. Celebrity fitness trainer Dino Nowak believes that lasting change must start from within. He likens the body's need for food to a car's need for gasoline. "If you keep trying to pump gas into your car and you're not driving it, you don't need that much gas. If you want to burn the gas, you have to drive the car."

"Do I *really* have to exercise?" I whine. The emphatic answer is, of course, *Yes!*

Through her book *Prayerwalking,* my good friend Janet Holm McHenry has influenced many by sharing how simple walks can revitalize both body and soul. Years ago when she was overweight and overstressed (an "undisciplined mess" in her own words), she began walking each morning through her neighborhood and praying for people and places she passed along the way. Not only has she seen others' lives changed by her constant and disciplined prayer for them, she has reaped incredible benefits as well.

One morning her teenager actually caught her singing while preparing his school lunch. "I, the one who had been depressed and whose usual morning words were solely along the lines of, 'Get up . . . I said get up . . . Get up or you'll be late,' was *singing.* God had been filling my soul while I prayerwalked, and I couldn't hold it in anymore. It occurred to me that my entire countenance—in fact my entire outlook on life—had changed. Prayerwalking an hour each weekday had transformed my life in just a couple of months."[7]

Often couch potatoes (of which I am a recovering one) have a mental block against any form of exercise. We conjure up images of sweating profusely, huffing and puffing, and generally finding the whole thing one big chore. We need to realize that exercise actually can be a spa for our soul. It literally does bring good and healthy feelings that affect all areas of our lives, as Janet discovered.

Leslie Sansone, author of *Walk Away the Pounds,* elaborated: "One of the best gifts God gave us was this gorgeous feeling of not only empowerment, but also the coping and peace that exercise brings us. And no drug, no pill, nothing takes the place of what our natural body produces when we are in motion, because God's design for muscle and bone is for them to be active. We're meant to be spiritual and physical beings, and when we're in motion we are happier, healthier, more creative and smarter."[8]

Perhaps you take yourself too seriously. Then it's time to lighten up, or as my teenager says, "Chill." Humor has a profoundly positive effect on our bodies. Laughter distracts us from pain by releasing endorphins that make us feel better and more alert. It increases blood circulation, lowers blood pressure, relieves muscle tension, eases stress, and makes us more relaxed. It revs up our body's ability to fight infection and clears mucus from our lungs. Truly, "a joyful heart is good medicine" (Prov. 17:22a).

We also need to be realistic about the changes we can and cannot make as we get older. Special challenges come as bodies age; disease sets in and women go through the change of life. God created women with bodies that procreate, and it's no wonder there is a sense of loss when one passes the season of giving birth. But we can embrace the change as a good thing and an opportunity for growth, just as Elyse did: "I stood before my mirror, hysterectomy scar still red, one breast stitched and swollen, dark blue and purple. What had happened to me? Was this still my body, or some alien thing bent on destroying me? In the past it had been my comfortable, although quirky, friend. I asked my reflection, 'Who am I, now? What am I, now? With so many parts gone, am I still a woman?' What is it that makes a woman womanly? God answered me and led me gradually to see my identity based on His blood, rather than my monthly blood. I am His child because He bled and died for me. I am a woman because He sculpted my heart and person this way, not because of my reproductive capabilities."[9]

While caring for our bodies is important, we also must realize a healthy body does not magically mean a healthy soul. One woman who survived cancer and is now embracing a new season of life said that learning to care for her soul was what healed her wounded self. "Grieve if you must, but be aware of an emerging wonderful reality—you are more than body, and new possibilities and potentials are opening to you. Care for your soul and you can be better at seventy than you were at seventeen. Care for your soul and you have made an enormous stride toward quality living. Care of the soul is the approach to aging that will help us manage the days to come with confidence, joy, and inner strength."[10]

Max Lucado tells the story of the two different house sitters. While the owner is gone, one sitter redecorates the whole house to his liking. When the owner returns, he says, "I asked you to take *care* of the house, not take *over* the house."

The other house sitter neglects the house—no cleaning, no repairs, no nothing. On the owner's return, the sitter exclaims, "My time here was temporary and I knew you wouldn't mind."

The problem with these two is that while they were house-sitting, they acted as if they owned the house. We do the same things with our bodies, act as if we own them, when God tells us differently. "Do you not know that your body is a sanctuary of the Holy Spirit who is in you, whom you have from God? You are not your own, for you were bought at a price; therefore glorify God in your body" (1 Cor. 6:19–20).[11]

Our physical bodies—tall or short, fat or skinny, lithe or bent— are Christ's tools for doing His work in the world. He has chosen to use us to further His kingdom here on earth. So our greatest response should be to offer our bodies back to Him to use as He will. "Therefore, brothers, by the mercies of God, I urge you to present your bodies as a living sacrifice, holy and pleasing to God; this is your spiritual worship" (Rom. 12:1).

No chapter on body image would be complete without some reference to sexuality. After all, God created us as sexual beings. However, with all the media hype about bodies beautiful, a natural preoccupation with sex has permeated our culture, often in quite damaging ways. I continue to be shocked and saddened at the blatant promiscuity that has come to be accepted as the norm. Raising four teenagers called for frequent conversation and discussion on the world's view of sex and sexuality. In the weekly teen girls Bible study I once led in my home —Girlz4God—we often prayed about these temptations and what God's Word says.

"Flee from sexual immorality! 'Every sin a person can commit is outside the body,' but the person who is sexually immoral sins against his own body" (1 Cor. 6:18). We discussed whether this meant to literally run. Sometimes, yes. But to stay away from temptation, we also must be careful how we dress, talk, and conduct ourselves and what we watch, listen to, and engage in.

"Sex was God's idea. From God's perspective, sex is nothing short of holy, a gift to be opened in a special place. That place is marriage. Sex outside of marriage pretends that we can give the body and not the soul. We can't. The me-centered phrase 'as long as no one gets hurt' sounds noble. The truth is, we don't know who gets hurt. Sex apart from God's plan wounds the soul. Sex according to God's plan nourishes the soul."[12]

As our bodies begin to break down, another common struggle is with coming to terms with aging or disability. And yet we are still commanded to use even this to strengthen our souls. "So remember your Creator in the days of your youth: Before the days of adversity come, and the years approach when you will say, 'I have no delight in them'" (Eccles. 12:1).

My friend Lael Arrington has had rheumatoid arthritis since age twenty-nine but daily inspires me with her vital ministry of writing and speaking about the Christian worldview, in spite of the increasing limitations of her body. She has learned we can glorify God in our bodies, no matter what their current condition. "I look back on years of suffering and realize that through 25 years of pain, limitation and loss, through a fractured hip, four joint replacements and bottles of tears, God has made my heart more and more beautiful as I have leaned on Him. He has torn into strongholds of pride and selfishness that were nourished by my health and outer beauty and is using the pain to make me his bride with a beautiful heart. Have you ever considered that, because of what God is doing through your pain, the real you is even more beautiful? God delights in our beauty and we can't help but enjoy Him in return."[13]

God longs to give us the kind of beauty not found in slick magazines but discovered on a journey through the pain and challenge of life. "The LORD has anointed me to . . . provide for those who mourn in Zion; to give them a crown of beauty instead of ashes, festive oil instead of mourning, and splendid clothes instead of despair" (Isa. 61:1, 3a).

The Bible doesn't dwell on how Jesus looked. In fact, our only glimpse is on his day of crucifixion: "He had no form or splendor that we should look at Him, no appearance that we should desire Him" (Isa. 53:2b). However, throughout Scripture we read of what Christ did with his body—touching, healing, speaking, feeding, building, fishing, eating, raising from the dead, and, of course, the ultimate, dying on a cross.

We can learn perspective about our own body's use by focusing on the fact that we are created in God's image in order to reflect His image. "There's no joy, no beauty, no celebration in preserving ourselves just to be ornamental. There is joy in being used, in becoming broken vessels, spilling out the fragrance of Christ on everyone we touch. There's fulfillment in dying to vanity and discovering real beauty's far more than looking good. True beauty is looking like Christ."[14]

During the past few years as my body has undergone radical changes, parts of it have rebelled. I know that hair loss and excess sagging skin are just two ways my body is reminding me it does not like change. In fact, experts say that whatever we stick to most consistently is where our body will cling. So, if I stay active and eat healthy natural foods, my body will adjust itself to that lifestyle. But if I stay sedentary and turn to food for emotional comfort, my body will adjust to that lifestyle.

Your soul is not so different. Whatever you do in your spiritual walk will reap benefits or consequences. Are you consistent with spending time with God, worshiping regularly, and reading your Bible? Or do you gravitate to people and activities that draw you away from the things of God? I recently read an article about Nick Yphantides, a medical doctor who lost 207 pounds by finally submitting himself and his habits to God. The doctor summed it up this way: "I discovered that you have to change the way you see before you can change the way you look." Romans 6:13b reminds us, "offer yourselves to God, and all the parts of yourselves to God as weapons for righteousness."

Spiritual Personal Assessment

Scripture. Read 1 Corinthians 6:19–20 and pray about what it means to live in a temple of the Holy Spirit. How can you be a good steward of your body and honor God through it?

Journal. Write down a few experiences or people who helped shape your body image early in life. Were they positive or negative influences? The three components of a healthy body image are respect, care, and perspective. Write each of these words in your private journal and then evaluate where you are currently in each area. How can you improve?

Discussion. If you could change one thing about your body, what would that be? Why? Is this kind of change within your power? If so, what do you have to do to get started? Go for it!

Which is hardest for you to do—eat wisely or exercise regularly? Can you pinpoint mental blocks to the action you know is right? Once you have targeted the hindrances, begin, one by one, to chip away at those and move forward toward greater health. Warning: this is a *process,* so begin with small victories each day and each week.

Spa Treatment. Be good to yourself and your body (God's temple) by seeking to follow these general health tips:

- Move! Each day find new ways to move your body. Use stairs, walk the dog, chase your kids, or mow the lawn. Anything that gets you off the couch is not only a fitness tool but a stress buster as well.

- Cut the fat! Try to avoid obvious fatty foods such as french fries and fatty meats. Eat low-fat versions of dairy products such as skim milk and cottage cheese. Limit margarine, sauces, and nuts.

- Reduce stress! Focus on positive things in your life and count your blessings. Do something you enjoy (walk on the beach, read a book, visit a friend, listen to soothing music, get a massage, watch a funny movie, ride a bike).

- Stop smoking! All experts agree on this.

- Wear your seat belt! This adds to longevity and helps alleviate potential injuries in car crashes.

- Limit alcohol! Too much drinking can cause serious health problems, such as liver and kidney disease and cancer.

- Think positive! There is a definite connection between living healthy and having a cheerful outlook. Keep smiling and laughing.

CHAPTER 5

Cardiotherapy

*"I will give you a new heart
and put a new spirit within you;
I will remove your heart of stone
and give you a heart of flesh."*

—Ezekiel 36:26

One year I spent Valentine's Day in the cardiac care unit of Hartford Hospital. This was not so I could literally have "Happy Heart Day." This was an emergency. My husband had failed his stress test and was discovered to have clogged arteries requiring heart catheterization. An angioplasty was performed to open his clogged artery, and a stent was put in to keep it open. This was a wake-up call for us. Since Mike looked extremely healthy and fit, we had no warning of impending heart disease. However, both his parents had suffered heart problems, so he was a prime candidate. After this procedure, we did all the "right" things. He was vigilant about the proper exercise, and we changed the way we ate. We were determined that this would lead him back to total heart wellness.

But it didn't. By Maundy Thursday of the same year, he was experiencing distress, and at the hospital it was discovered the stent had already occluded. The cardiologist came to me in the waiting room and said he needed to know the name of our heart surgeon.

"I don't have a heart surgeon!" I exclaimed.

"Well, I need a name in the next ten minutes. Mike is scheduled for a five-way bypass tomorrow," he said and left me.

I called friends Ed and Bill who gave me the names of three top heart surgeons in our area. Fortunately, the first one on the list was available, and we were set for open-heart surgery on Good Friday. The irony was not lost on us as Mike's life was placed on the heart and lung machine at the same time (3 p.m.) our church was keeping vigil at the cross during the Good Friday service.

This Easter we celebrated Mike's fifteen healthy years since heart surgery. We are grateful he is doing well, actually better than before! And we are both on a more deliberate path to living healthier lives as a result of our wake-up call with heart disease.

I was shocked to learn recently that heart disease is the number-one killer of women today. I believe we need to take this seriously, and I have included education and prevention in this chapter. But I also believe that "heartsickness" is a devastating factor in the lives of women today. Too many women I encounter are slowly dying from anger, unforgiveness, and stress. They, too, need cardiotherapy from the Great Physician.

One of the first steps is to recognize there is a need. I'm grateful that former President George W. Bush signed a presidential proclamation declaring February American Heart Month. This was in recognition of the important ongoing fight against heart disease, and the valentine season is an appropriate time of year to remind us.

Former First Lady Laura Bush was also instrumental with the American Heart Association in launching a nationwide campaign to raise awareness that heart disease is women's number one killer. While red is a symbol for women and heart disease, it also symbolizes the power of women investing in their heart health. National Wear Red Day supports the red dress as the national symbol for women and heart disease awareness. On the first Friday in February each year, women and men across the country unite in the national movement to give women a personal and urgent wake-up call about their risk of heart disease. Many women and men participate in this lifesaving awareness movement by showing off a favorite red dress, shirt, or tie. I have personally bought several red-dress pins to wear and give to girlfriends.

"*The Heart Truth* is that heart disease is the #1 killer of American women. In fact, one in three women dies of heart disease. But heart disease also can lead to disability and a significantly decreased quality of life. Unfortunately, most women don't know this and rarely take their risk of heart disease seriously—or personally. Women often fail to make the connection between risk factors, such as high blood pressure and high cholesterol, and their own chance of developing heart disease."[1]

Having a healthy cardiovascular system, which supplies blood and oxygen to every part of the body, is the key to living a long and energetic life. Cardiovascular disease is mostly preventable, so understanding these serious health threats can make a lifesaving difference.

According to the American Heart Association, major risk factors for heart disease include a family history of heart disease, age, being male, smoking, high cholesterol, high blood pressure, not exercising, diabetes, and being overweight or obese. The more risk factors you have, the greater your chances for heart attack or stroke. According to the National Institute of Health, women whose waist measures more than thirty-five inches and men whose waists are more than forty inches are more likely to be at risk for heart disease than their trimmer counterparts.[2]

But what about the disease of *heartsickness*? What about those who are heavyhearted or hard-hearted? Throughout the Psalms we read of such situations: "I am poured out like water, and all my bones are disjointed; my heart is like wax, melting within me" (Ps. 22:14). "I am faint and severely crushed; I groan because of the anguish of my heart" (Ps. 38:8). "For troubles without number have surrounded me; my sins have overtaken me; I am unable to see. They are more than the hairs of my head, and my courage leaves me" (Ps. 40:12). "My spirit is weak within me; my heart is overcome with dismay" (Ps. 143:4).

The psalmist voiced what many women feel today—brokenhearted. Whether it is from a death of dreams, pain, discouragement, or rejection, hearts are fragile and any number of things can wield the final blow. I read in *Time* magazine that someone can actually die from a broken heart! The *New England Journal of Medicine* reported that physicians at Johns Hopkins University now consider a broken heart a real medical event, one that can kill.

"A group of 18 mostly older women and one man developed serious heart problems after experiencing a sudden emotional shock, such as the death of a loved one, or, in the case of one 60-year-old woman, a surprise birthday party." None of these people actually suffered a heart attack. Few had any signs of heart disease at all. What doctors did find was elevated levels of stress hormones—up to thirty-four times as great as normal levels. "It's still unclear whether the hormones caused the cardiac problems or were caused by them. Nor can doctors explain why women's hearts seem more vulnerable than men since men typically produce higher levels of those stress hormones than women do." The good news is that what doctors now call the broken-heart syndrome is reversible, provided the initial shock isn't too great.[3]

God wants us to be heart healthy. Throughout the Bible are accusations of people being hard-hearted. In the Old Testament God called the Israelites hard-hearted, and in the New Testament Jesus warned the religious leaders. Hard-hearted refers to the unresponsive, stiff, angry, insensitive, rebellious, and independent attitudes ruling our hearts. Even in Jesus' parable of the sower (Mark 4), seed thrown on hard-packed soil didn't grow. When Jesus interpreted this parable, He likened that soil to the hearts of some who were impenetrable, hardened, unresponsive, and callous. The Word can never take root in such conditions.

Today, many symptoms of hard-heartedness are such things as erecting walls to protect us from pain, living with an "It's all about me" attitude, refusing to give God lordship and control over our behavior, and harboring pain and grudges. All of these hurt us and can damage our souls.

According to Ezekiel, idolatry was the cause of hardened hearts, and God desired to replace the idolatry of the Israelites. "And I will give them one heart and put a new spirit within them; I will remove their heart of stone from their bodies and give them a heart of flesh" (Ezek. 11:19). Most of us don't think of ourselves as idol worshipers in the twenty-first century, but we are. Whenever we focus on what we get by serving God (good luck, prosperity, long life, success in battle, power, or prestige), we are not worshiping Him simply for who He is. That is what the idols of long ago did for the people. They believed one idol brought rain, another fertility. All of them were means to a desired end.

But God wants to *change* our hearts, to replace the heart of stone with a heart of flesh. He said to His people, "If you return, Israel—[this is] the Lord's declaration—[if] you return to Me, if you remove your detestable idols from My presence and do not waver, if you swear, As the Lord lives, in truth, in justice, and in righteousness, then the nations will be blessed by Him and will pride themselves in Him" (Jer. 4:1–2).

King David, a former shepherd, put it this way: "For He is our God, and we are the people of His pasture, the sheep under His care. Today, if you hear His voice: 'Do not harden your hearts'" (Ps. 95:7–8a). My friend Paula Rinehart, author of *Strong Women, Soft Hearts,* felt awed to observe women who chose to live with new hearts, vulnerable and open to what God can do. "The strength of vulnerability is a curious mixture of discovering your heart and sharing your real self, as best you can, with the people God has put in your life. You can't shut down on the inside without quelling the very passion that makes the journey worthwhile. Those walls around the heart take buckets of energy to maintain, and God has better things for His children to do. When we close off our hearts we dishonor Him. As difficult as it is to live with a vulnerable heart, it is far easier than camping out behind a façade."[4]

We must be willing to let go in order to heal. In my book *Amazed by Grace,* I shared in the chapter "Astonished by Sin" that when I was younger I had to be confronted with my own anger, which was a symptom of unnamed sins—pride, lack of trust in God, self-centeredness. My sin was blatant every time I chose to go my way and not God's way. Why trust when I could worry? Why surrender when I could control? Why show compassion when I could stand in judgment? Why accept responsibility when I could blame others?

Have you ever sinned against the Lord through your anger? God knows that within our emotional makeup is anger, but the Bible says, "Be angry and do not sin. Don't let the sun go down on your anger" (Eph. 4:26). While that verse acknowledges that we can expect to experience anger, it also points out that how we handle anger determines whether or not it will lead to sin. During my own pilgrimage this poem by Jessica Shaver helped me understand how heart cleansing can occur:

A Prayer for Freedom

I told God I was angry. I thought He'd be surprised.
I thought I'd kept hostility quite cleverly disguised.
I told the Lord I hated Him. I told Him that I hurt.
I told Him that it isn't fair. He's treated me like dirt.
I told God I was angry, but I'm the one surprised.
"What I've known all along," He said, "you've finally realized."
"At last you have admitted what's really in your heart.
Dishonesty, not anger, was keeping us apart.
"Even when you hate me I don't stop loving you.
Before you can receive that love you must confess what's true
"In telling me the anger you genuinely feel
it loses power over you, permitting you to heal."
I told God I was sorry and He's forgiven me,
The truth that I was angry has finally set me free.[5]

For many of us, an unforgiving spirit has seized our hearts and hardened them. We are only hurting ourselves, keeping us in a prison of our own making. Lewis Smedes, author of *Forgive and Forget,* pointed out, "Every time we forgive, we set a prisoner free and the prisoner we set free is ourselves." He further elaborated on three steps to every act of forgiveness:

1. See the offender as a flawed human being just like ourselves.

2. Surrender our precious right to get even with him and choose to live with the scales unbalanced.

3. Gradually find the will to wish him well.

"Once begun—and remember this is almost always a process, sometimes a lifelong journey—we are open to whatever our future holds and we can have hope again. People who discover the grace to forgive almost always discover the grace of hope besides.

> *Those walls around the heart take buckets of energy to maintain and God has better things for His children to do.*
> —Paula Rinehart,
> *Strong Women, Soft Hearts*

"Hopegiving forgiveness happens totally inside the victim who does the forgiving. The good news is that even if we cannot be reconciled to the other person, we have by forgiving him created hope for ourselves. To forgive is to unglue ourselves from the bad things people did to us yesterday. And to free ourselves from the bad things we did to others or ourselves. Becoming a more forgiving person always, not sometimes, but always turns us into a more hopeful person."[6]

In Colossians 1:13, Paul stated that God has "rescued us from the domain of darkness and transferred us into the kingdom of the Son He loves." Have you been rescued from the dominion of darkness? Do you need to be?

I love the old story of the grave-digger who finished preparing an open grave for a funeral the next day but then found he could not climb out of the deep hole. He tried everything to no avail, then decided to curl up in a corner and sleep there until the next day when someone would come to help. Around midnight when it was pitch dark, a drunk wandered into the cemetery and fell into the open grave, which awakened the sleeping man in the corner. Of course, the drunk, scared to death to be all alone in the pit of a dark grave, tried desperately to climb out but was just as unsuccessful as the gravedigger. Just then he heard a deep voice behind him say, "You'll never get out of this grave." But he did!

Would that adrenaline or fear or whatever could propel us as quickly out of the darkness in which we often find ourselves.

Just as my husband's clogged arteries had to be bypassed with new arteries, so our souls also must be healed from heart disease. According to heart specialist Dr. Dean Ornish, the real epidemic people face today is emotional and spiritual heart disease—loneliness and isolation. He says we are losing the relationships and intimacy necessary for our survival and healing—the social support that provides us with a sense of connection and community and also the emotional support that gives us a sense of purpose, meaning, and belonging.[7] When we close our hearts, we cut off all connection to others who may be helpful in our healing process. A closed heart lessens our risks but narrows our options.

A *Spa* magazine even touted these benefits. "In the lifelong pursuit of mind and body well-being, don't overlook forgiveness—it's as beneficial as yoga or a good night's sleep. Research suggests that the release of negative emotions can unravel the effects of stress, helping to alleviate depression, boost the immune system, and improve cardiovascular health. Often even when the act of forgiveness doesn't entail reconciliation or forgetting past wrongs, it helps others understand that these events can't hurt them today. As one Spa doctor says, 'The more you forgive, the more you live—literally.'"[8]

God promises to renew our hearts. "I will give them a heart to know Me, that I am the LORD. They will be My people, and I will be their God because they will return to Me with all their heart" (Jer. 24:7). Then we no longer have to focus on what has kept us emotionally or spiritually clogged. Listen to one woman's declaration of independence: "I am not a woman who is conformed to my pain, whose self definition is the litany of sins that has been committed against me, who would have little left if were I to lose it [my pain]. No. I am a woman whose soul is forming to God. I cannot control how others treat me, but I can control my own response. I choose to relate to others based on my own character, not theirs. That is a tremendously freeing concept! My soul, formed in its becoming to the dimensions of God's love, can extend forgiveness, even when the other person is not worthy, never says the word sorry or ever shows a grain of remorse. My offender has no power over me. I hurt, but do not become stuck there. I grow beyond the break and eventually past the power of the pain."

We are never truly alone in the journey, and it's always important to share community in our search for heart health. For about ten years I was part of a wonderful group of twelve women speakers from New England who prayed regularly for each other and met annually for a weekend retreat of prayer and conversation. Our name was Heartspring, based on two key Scriptures: "for his mouth speaks from the overflow of the heart" (Luke 6:45b) and "Above all else, guard your heart, for it is the wellspring of life" (Prov. 4:23 NIV). We covenanted to keep each other accountable as sisters in the Lord so our hearts would be in the right place. For what was in our hearts (or *not* in our hearts) would spring forth and directly affect our speaking ministries.

This was a precious group, but like many good things, it was not sustained forever. Half of the women moved out of the region, and it became impossible to maintain the close bonds of prayer and support. Recently we had a wonderful reunion in Boston. And I still feel a deep bond of sisterhood whenever I'm with one of the Heartspringers. I'm still convinced we need others to help us in our cardiotherapy.

I began this chapter with a medical crisis in our family—my husband's heart surgery. There are three possible outcomes of any crisis: a change for the better, a change for the worse, or a return to the previous level of functioning. When a doctor talks about a crisis, she talks about the moment in the course of the disease when a change for the better or worse occurs. When a counselor talks about a marital crisis, she talks about the turning point when the marriage can go in either direction—toward growth, enrichment, and improvement or toward dissatisfaction, pain, and possible dissolution.

Most of us desire that the outcome is for the better, but do we realize that much of that depends on our own attitude? The Chinese term for crisis *(weji)* is made up of two symbols—one for "danger" and the other for "opportunity." The English word is based on the Greek word *krinein,* meaning "to decide." So every crisis is a time of decision. Yes, it is dangerous, but it is also an opportunity.

The state of your heart—your soul—is all important. It helps determine who you are and how you'll live out your days here on earth. Is your heart totally sold out to God? Are you seeking His will and His way in every decision of life? What do you need to do to exchange your heart of stone for a heart of flesh?

One book that affected me profoundly in the past decade was *The Sacred Romance* by John Eldredge and the late Brent Curtis. And I believe the reason is because their words penetrated my aching, needy heart that desperately wanted to hear how God tenderly woos and romances me with His love. Their words struck a chord. "The inner life, the story of our heart, is the life of the deep places within us, our passions and dreams, our fears and our deepest wounds. . . . The heart does not respond to principles and programs; it seeks not efficiency but passion."[9]

At my age and stage of life, I think a lot about legacy. I realize that in the end it doesn't really matter how well I have performed or what I have accomplished, even for God. But it would matter if I left my heart behind. A life without heart is not worth living. "For out of this wellspring of our soul flows all true caring and all meaningful work, all real worship and all sacrifice. Our faith, hope, and love issue from this fount, as well. Because it is in our *hearts* that we first hear the voice of God and it is in the heart that we come to know Him and learn to live in His love."[10]

Spiritual Personal Assessment

Scripture. Read Proverbs 4:23 and pray about those words of admonition. How can you guard your heart? If your heart is the wellspring of life, what does the current state of your heart say about your life?

Journal. Write down anything that you believe is clogging your heart. Be sure to list old grievances you are still holding, people and situations that continue to anger you, and unconfessed sins. Write it all down (remember, this is your private journal). Then offer all these situations to God in an act of relinquishment. Confess to Him and pray that He will cleanse you and help you to live in the freedom He longs to give you. Then take a long walk—that's also good for your heart!

Discussion. Are you currently suffering from the disease of heartsickness or hard-heartedness? If so, how is this manifested in your life (depression, avoiding others, doubting God's presence)? What can you do today to begin a process of healing your heart?

Have you ever had a broken heart? Did you learn anything during that time of pain? How did you experience healing from your brokenness?

Spa Treatment. Cardio workout: Your body's best time for cardio is late afternoon, according to a study from the Long Island Jewish Medical Center in New York. A significant drop in airway resistance around this time of day allows exercisers to absorb as much as 15 to 20 percent more air than normal. Apparently, lung function has its own circadian rhythm, which peaks between 4 and 5 p.m. and dips around noon. Still, the best time to work out is the one you can fit most consistently into your schedule.

Know your numbers! Then do whatever it takes to keep them at a healthy level. Here are four key numbers for preventing heart disease and diabetes:

1. Blood sugar or blood glucose level: Ideally, it should be between 65 and 110.

2. Blood pressure: A good reading is 120 over 80, although experts are now pushing for even lower numbers.

3. Cholesterol level: The total should be under 200. The "good" cholesterol (or HDL) should be over 40—the higher the better. The "bad" cholesterol (LDL) should be under 100.

4. Weight: If you want to focus on lowering one of these four numbers, start here. If you reduce your weight, the other areas will follow.

CHAPTER 6

Extreme Makeover

So here's what I want you to do, God helping you:
Take your everyday, ordinary life—your sleeping, eating, going-
to-work, and walking-around life—and place it before God as an
offering. Embracing what God does for you is the best thing you
can do for him. Don't become so well-adjusted to your culture that
you fit into it without even thinking. Instead, fix your attention
on God. You'll be changed from the inside out. Readily recognize
what he wants from you, and quickly respond to it. Unlike the
culture around you, always dragging you down to its level of
immaturity, God brings the best out of you, develops well-formed
maturity in you.

—ROMANS 12:1–2 MSG

Our culture, for better or for worse, is reflected in the media through television programs. For several years now we have experienced the fad of reality TV. I don't know whose reality these endless shows about dating, mating, fear, and survival are supposed to depict, but it's certainly not my life! A few years ago my teenager and I happened to watch a then new reality show called *Extreme Makeover,* and it was a real eye-opener!

The show's premise was that someone wants desperately to change her looks in every way. The change is always a combination of many things—weight, hair, teeth, eyes, chin, face, wardrobe. A wealthy television executive says, "Sign here on the dotted line and we will make you perfect! Just trust us." During the ensuing hour, we observe the participant go through all kinds of procedures until "the big reveal," when the made-over person parades in front of her family and friends who ooh and aah over the remarkable changes.

And they truly are remarkable. People loved this show. Hey, I was even drawn to this show, though it seemed like voyeurism. There's nothing wrong with looking your best. I'm the first to agree we should shine for Christ. But I have a deeper problem with this infatuation with makeovers and especially plastic surgery: Is it only skin deep? What happens to the person on the *inside* once she has been extremely made-over on the *outside*?

We cannot separate the two. We are souls living inside bodies, and each affects the other. On my own journey toward better health, I've been forced to make radical choices to mentally change the way I view food and exercise. I've also had to examine my own soul for deeper reasons that contributed to unhealthy behavior.

Spiritually I've discovered that God is the One who wants to perform an extreme makeover on each of us! Are there areas in your life you'd like to change? Subtractions? Additions? Don't go to television. And don't go to the plastic surgeon. Go to the divine Physician, the One who said through the prophet Isaiah, "Do not remember the past events, pay no attention to things of old. Look, I am about to do something new; even now it is coming. Do you not see it? Indeed, I will make a way in the wilderness, rivers in the desert" (Isa. 43:18–19).

How encouraged are you to know God is doing a new thing in your life? I believe no matter what your age or stage in life, it is never too late to write the story of the rest of your life. True, you can't go back and redo what has happened thus far, but you can have a new beginning. God also speaks to this in the New Testament through the apostle Paul who experienced an extreme makeover from being the number one Pharisee persecutor of Christians to the number one apostle of the good news of grace and transformation: "Brothers, I do not consider myself to have taken hold of it. But one thing I do: forgetting what is behind and reaching forward to what is ahead, I pursue as my goal the prize promised by God's heavenly call in Christ Jesus" (Phil. 3:13–14).

I was thinking of this passage on the first Sunday of the new year when I read the comic pages and noticed that *Peanuts* portrayed what many of us feel when faced with new beginnings.

Charlie Brown approaches Lucy, holding out a piece of paper. "I've decided that this next year is going to be my year of decision! This is the list of things in my life that I'm going to correct. . . . I'm going to be a better person!"

But Lucy, ever the pessimist, replies, "Not me. I'm going to spend this whole year regretting the past. It's the only way, Charlie Brown. I'm going to cry over spilt milk, and sigh over lost loves. It's a lot easier. It's hard to improve. I tried it once and it drove me crazy. 'Forget the Future' is my motto. 'Regret the Past.'"

Most of us are torn between desires for change and thoughts of the past that immobilize us. Lucy is right—it is hard to improve! But Charlie Brown is right, too—we have a year of decision to be a better person!

The hard part is finding the balance between looking ahead to our potential and trying to learn from past mistakes. While journeying through life, I've discovered it's quite difficult driving my car without an occasional glance in the rearview mirror to check where I've been. However, for most of the journey my eyes need to look ahead, alert to unexpected encounters and directional signs. I wouldn't get far if I concentrated solely on what was already behind me.

And yet, any new beginning can sometimes be thwarted by unresolved baggage from the past. That's why we must keep short accounts with others and with God. Do you believe God will forgive your past sins and regrets if you offer them to Him in an act of repentance? God's Word proclaims it: "If we confess our sins, He is faithful and righteous to forgive us our sins and to cleanse us from all unrighteousness" (1 John 1:9).

Do you also believe there is hope for lasting change and transformation for those who put themselves in God's hands? Hear another of God's promises: "For I know the plans I have for you"—[this is] the LORD's declaration—"plans for [your] welfare, not for disaster, to give you a future and a hope" (Jer. 29:11).

Whatever change you desire, whatever new beginning—whether it be a new year, a new program of recovery, or a new relationship—who will you choose to be, Charlie Brown or Lucy? How about neither? Be *yourself!* But choose to change.

Yes, we each have a choice. This morning when you woke up, some of you said, "Good morning, God!" and some of you said, "Good God, it's morning!" Which one are you?

I once stood in Old Jerusalem overlooking the ruins of the Pool of Bethesda and read aloud the story Jesus told of the crippled man who had lain for thirty-eight years by the pool. (This story is found in John 5.1-15) He hoped that someone would carry him to the healing waters when the waters were stirred. That was lots of waiting—lots of time to be miserable and think about his illness and helplessness. But then Jesus came, and what did He say to this man?

"Do you want to get well?"

What kind of a question is that? I can just hear the guy saying, "Duh?" But actually it's a good question for us today too. Do we *want* to change? Because sometimes we get so used to being the way we are, warts and all, or we get so used to our pain that it becomes part of our identity. We don't know who we'd be without it. And as bad as it may be, as painful, discouraging, or even disgusting as we may be, sometimes we cling to the known, rather than risk the unknown.

One woman named Karen learned this lesson. "Change and growth can be exhilarating when we rely on His guidance and power to make a way when there seems to be no way. I didn't trust Him because I didn't know Him. I didn't know Him because I didn't read His Word. I didn't pray until I was desperate, and I didn't realize that if I had prayed every day, I probably wouldn't have gotten so desperate in the first place. . . . If I could do one thing over, a decade ago I would have slowed down long enough to take an honest look at my life. I would have asked God to join me in that process. And I would have *chosen to risk change instead of selling out to the familiar*—my fear, my pride, and my busyness."

Change is nearly always difficult, even when it's a chosen and desired change. I still remember the newness of my very first laptop computer. My middle children – Tim and Fiona – wanted to help me in my writing, so one Christmas they bought me a laptop computer. I was thrilled because my old computer was ancient. Nonetheless, it was a daunting task to learn the ropes on the new computer and begin using new files, new e-mail, and new hookups. The laptop was worlds better than my clunker desktop, and yet I found myself at times returning to the old computer merely because it was more familiar.

"Mom, don't use that old computer! Use the new one!" Tim exclaimed when I phoned him a week or so later with a technology question. "I don't want to hear again that you're on the old computer." So I weaned myself from it, and now I can't imagine using anything else.

Do you *want* to change? If you really want a different life, the choice is yours. "I call heaven and earth as witnesses against you today that I have set before you life and death, blessing and curse. Choose life so that you and your descendants may live" (Deut. 30:19).

In *Man's Search for Meaning*, Viktor Frankl's powerful book about his experience in a concentration camp, he wrote: "Every freedom was taken from us, except the last freedom, which is the freedom to choose one's attitude, to choose one's own way."

We choose with our minds first. If the battle is won there, the rest follows. So choose life! Choose transformation. That's the word for major change. To be not only polished on the outside, but to be totally made-over, beginning within. And that's the kind of change Jesus brings to us.

I recently read a magazine from the Chicago area in which one editor was lamenting reality TV. She was tired of what she was seeing and asked why the changes on the shows couldn't be more radical. "I want to see dramatic alteration—the kind that takes a son-of-a-gun who shouts at blind ladies crossing streets to hurry up, and morphs him into a compassionate prince who rescues kittens from trees, works weekends for the homeless, calls his mother regularly and sends money to save the rain forest." In other words, radical change.

She even used biblical terms. "I'm talking spiritual transformation, life-altering behavioral modification. Personality Boot Camp for Swine. Basically, I want to see the 21st-century version of Ebenezer Scrooge, where a real you-know-what gets some visitors and suddenly realizes life would go much more smoothly and be far more gratifying in the end if only he were a whole lot nicer. I envision the makeover of a horror-of-a-human by a barrage of psychiatrists, life coaches, spouses, children and friends with a few visits from the other side thrown in for good measure. The end result would be to transform Swine into Saint." She concluded, "We are a culture of *befores* longing to be *afters*."[1]

When candidates applied to be on *Extreme Makeover*, they had to plead their case so that the show would take on their challenge. If chosen, many resources were expended in their direction in order to assure a dramatic and complete change. One show executive stated, "We don't want someone who just needs a tweak here and there. We want someone who needs radical transformation." That is what attracts many viewers. Those on *Extreme Makeover* submit themselves to the authority of the experts who decide on tummy tucks, Lasik eye surgery, cosmetic dentistry, hair color, and a complete fashion redo. The whole point is to effect a major change. How absurd it would be if a client simply refused to follow the directions of the expert!

What does it take for *us* to finally come before God and plead our case for an extreme makeover? First, we must recognize our great need— that there is deep within us a desperation to *not stay the same.* We no longer want to live the way we have always lived. It's not enough anymore! We're finally tired of looking for love in all the wrong places; of living from crisis to crisis; of fearing, worrying, and carrying trunk loads of shame, guilt, and unmet expectations. When we've finally had enough and want change enough, we will do whatever is needed to submit to the Expert.

Are you ready to make that choice?

You make choices every day of your life, and many choices have consequences but not irrevocable ones. For instance, you can choose to accept the wrong kind of job and even though you may encounter all kinds of problems, it probably won't be the end of the world. You can even choose to live in a less than desirable place and find yourself in a bad situation, but that, too, can be remedied without too much fallout. You can choose to spend money foolishly or date the wrong kind of guy or give yourself a home perm, but you'll survive!

> *We are a culture of* befores *longing to be* afters.
> —MICHELE WELDON

But, dear sisters, there is one choice you better get right. And that is this one: What are you going to do about Jesus? How important is God in your life? Will you surrender your whole self (body, mind, and spirit) to Him and allow Him to change you from the inside out? If you miss the right choice here (Deuteronomy calls it choosing death instead of life, curses instead of blessings), you're in for a heap of sorrow. Your whole future is in jeopardy. And your present doesn't look so hot either.

Do you want to get well? Do you want to change? Do you want an extreme makeover, deep cleansing, and a new beginning? If so, you can't be halfhearted; you must go for it with your whole heart. In *The Weight of Glory,* C. S. Lewis made this observation: "We are half-hearted creatures, fooling about with drink and sex and ambition when infinite JOY is offered to us. Like an ignorant child who wants to go on making mud pies in a slum because he cannot imagine what is meant by the offer of a holiday at the sea. We are far too easily pleased."

"OK, Cindy," you say, "I'd love to change, and not just my looks either. I'd love to become a godly woman who just oozes patience, hope, and confidence, but hello, where in the world do I begin?"

We begin with God's Word, specifically chapter 12 of Paul's letter to the Romans. "Therefore, brothers, by the mercies of God, I urge you to present your bodies as a living sacrifice, holy and pleasing to God; this is your spiritual worship. Do not be conformed to this age, but be transformed by the renewing of your mind, so that you may discern what is the good, pleasing, and perfect will of God" (vv. 1–2).

How well I remember studying about offering myself as a "living sacrifice, holy and pleasing to God" while in seminary only to have a visiting professor, Dr. John R. W. Stott, make a point I have never forgotten. "The problem with living sacrifices is that they keep crawling off the altar!" I don't know if it was his words or the distinguished British accent of a brilliant man delivering those words, but they have checked me many a time as I have begun to crawl off the altar.

The original language of the New Testament was Greek. The Greek word used in the above verses is *metamorphoo* from which we get *metamorphosis* in English. Paul used a variant of that word in Galatians 4:19: "until Christ is formed in you." Here *metamorphoo* is translated into our English word *transformation*. The transformation God desires for us is a process of morphing into Christ likeness. It means a total change from one thing to a distinct other.

Do you remember a children's cartoon from the early 1980s, *The Mighty Morphin Power Rangers*? The teenage characters on this show would yell, "It's morphing time," and then they would receive power to do extraordinary things. Sometimes I can just hear the Lord saying to me, "It's morphing time!" He wants to give me power to do extraordinary things, but I have to respond.

Perhaps the easiest way to understand metamorphosis is the example of the butterfly. It begins life as a caterpillar—a squishy, squirmy, slimy thing crawling around on the ground. All it can do is crawl, but it doesn't know anything different so I assume it's happy. That is, until nature takes over and it finds itself in a surprising place—tight, dark, and scary. In fact, it feels a lot like death. We know it as a chrysalis or cocoon; the caterpillar sees it simply as the end of its world. But important things are happening during this process.

After a period of time, the caterpillar begins to break through the covering, first a little hole, then a bigger one, and it finally emerges. During this struggle a secretion is released that gives the ability to stretch its new wings and fly. Unfortunately, if there were no struggle to emerge, there would also be no soaring. Were we to discover the butterfly breaking through the cocoon and rescue it by cutting the cocoon open, it would never fly, because one important step would have been bypassed—the struggle.

Now it has metamorphosed into a totally different creature. It is not merely a prettier caterpillar that crawls faster. It is a wholly new creation—a butterfly with gorgeous markings and these incredible things called wings that enable it to fly and see more and be more. This is the kind of transformation God calls us to in Romans 12! Not just a better version of our *old* self. Not just tucked, lifted, veneered, and dyed, but *changed*—an extreme makeover from the inside out.

"Assuming you heard Him and were taught by Him, because the truth is in Jesus: you took off your former way of life, the old man that is corrupted by deceitful desires; you are being renewed in the spirit of your minds; you put on the new man, the one created according to God's [likeness] in righteousness and purity of the truth" (Eph. 4:21–24).

This whole idea of change is both our part and God's part through the power of the Holy Spirit. Don't rely on merely one of those by saying, "It's all up to me!" with a checklist of what to do. Neither should you sit back and say, "It's all up to God."

The important thing to remember from both Romans 12 and Ephesians 4 is that we are called to begin with a renewal of our *minds.* Ephesians 4:23 says, "You are being renewed in the spirit of your minds." This is both a once-and-for-all decision when we first accept Christ as our Lord and Savior, and it's also a daily commitment. We are not to be driven by desire and impulse, but we are to head in a totally new direction governed by our new way of thinking and empowered by the Holy Spirit.

Not conforming to the world is much more than just outward morality or keeping the rules. The summer I was twenty years old I worked as a missionary in the poverty-stricken Appalachian Mountains of Kentucky. One of the many things I learned that summer was that outward morality doesn't always equal inner godliness. Many of the fundamentalist churches frowned on women wearing sleeveless shirts, and yet incest was rampant within their ranks. Change must penetrate our minds, hearts, and souls because otherwise it is possible to stay proud, covetous, stubborn, and arrogant inside. Only the Holy Spirit can renew, reeducate, and redirect our minds and help us be truly transformed.

"For those whose lives are according to the flesh think about the things of the flesh, but those whose lives are according to the Spirit, about the things of the Spirit. For the mind-set of the flesh is death, but the mind-set of the Spirit is life and peace" (Rom. 8:5–6). But how are we to become women controlled by the Spirit when everything else in our world is clamoring for control of our minds and energies? The only way to grow in godliness is through the age-old spiritual disciplines of prayer, Bible study, worship, fasting, witness, and giving.

I spent much of my life *trying,* or perhaps I should say *striving,* to live a godly life and make myself the kind of person worthy of God's love and grace until I discovered the very nature of grace is that it is

God's gift to those who don't deserve it and can never earn it. It is a gift, not a reward. One of the very reasons you need a spa for your soul and are reading this book is that perhaps you, too, are weary of trying so hard. The good news is that you can change, and it will take effort on your part, but you have a partner with the Holy Spirit.

Since we can't actually make transformation happen to us since it is something God does, what is our role in the process? John Ortberg said,

> Training means arranging life around those activities that enable us to do what we cannot do now, even by extreme effort. Significant human transformation always involves training, not just trying. As we train ourselves in godliness, we begin to overcome the limits of sinful patterns. The purpose of that discipline is always freedom—training myself to be free of the obstacles that hinder my transformation.
>
> Spiritual transformation is a long-term endeavor. It involves both God and us. I liken it to crossing an ocean. Some people try, day after day, to be good, to become spiritually mature. That's like taking a rowboat across the ocean. It's exhausting and usually unsuccessful.
>
> Others have given up trying and throw themselves entirely on "relying on God's grace." They're like drifters on a raft. They do nothing but hang on and hope God gets them there.
>
> Neither trying nor drifting is very effective in bringing about spiritual transformation. A better image is the sailboat, in which if it moves at all, it's a gift of the wind. We can't control the wind, but a good sailor discerns where the wind is blowing and adjusts the sails accordingly.
>
> Working with the Holy Spirit, which Jesus likened to the wind in John 3, means we have a part in discerning the winds, in knowing the direction we need to go, and in training our sails to catch the breezes that God provides. That's true transformation.[2]

The overhaul of your soul begins with making a choice to change, to be willing to let go of the safe and familiar and take a risk for the new person God intends you to be. Next, your mind must be redesigned to reflect godliness more than worldliness. This takes discipline and daily renewal through prayer and obedience to what God desires. And remember, this is a lifetime process! Finally, you must realize that only through the power of the Holy Spirit can true change be accomplished. Therefore, live in partnership with the Spirit.

I began this chapter by taking to task the reality show *Extreme Makeover*. But I recently read the testimony of a Christian woman who was a contestant on that show. Cynthia Lunceford of Louisiana was born with nerve deafness and was also losing her sight by age forty. And she needed her eyes to read lips!

This former Campus Crusade staff worker had one of the most successful makeovers on the show. She received dental restoration, digital hearing aids, Lasik eye surgery, and more. Yet Cynthia was quick to say, "Without my having a relationship with Jesus Christ, the *Extreme Makeover* team could have given me a perfect body and it would not have made me happy, satisfied or able to get to heaven. It was like God looked at me and said, 'You already had the ultimate extreme makeover in what you received when you accepted my Son.' The physical *Extreme Makeover* on the outside was nothing compared to the spiritual extreme makeover I had on the inside. Our earthly bodies decay, but our spirits can be transformed to last forever."

Cynthia wrote in her journal, "This started out as a wild and crazy adventure and it ended up a grand and grace-filled experience." With newfound confidence, she is now using this experience to present the gospel to large groups. "Whereas the average unbeliever might not be interested in going to church or hearing a spiritual message, the makeover is like a hook that captures their interest. It's an incredible reality that God uses us to bring people into His kingdom."[3]

As God performs an extreme makeover on us from the inside out, we are empowered to live for Him in a fresh, new way. To this end we can live out Paul's word in Romans 12:9–21:

> *Love must be without hypocrisy. Detest evil; cling to what is good. Show family affection to one another with brotherly love. Outdo one another in showing honor. Do not lack diligence; be fervent in spirit; serve the Lord. Rejoice in hope; be patient in affliction; be persistent in*

prayer. Share with the saints in their needs; pursue hospitality. Bless those who persecute you; bless and do not curse. Rejoice with those who rejoice; weep with those who weep. Be in agreement with one another. Do not be proud; instead, associate with the humble. Do not be wise in your own estimation. Do not repay anyone evil for evil. Try to do what is honorable in everyone's eyes. If possible, on your part, live at peace with everyone. Friends, do not avenge yourselves; instead, leave room for His wrath. For it is written: Vengeance belongs to Me; I will repay, says the Lord. But

> *If your enemy is hungry, feed him.*
> *If he is thirsty, give him something to drink.*
> *For in so doing you will be heaping fiery coals on his head.*
> *Do not be conquered by evil, but conquer evil with good.*

We can't change ourselves, but we can work in partnership with our Creator and move from crawling to soaring. It's morphing time!

Spiritual Personal Assessment

Scripture. Read the whole chapter of Romans 12 in your own Bible, underlining Paul's phrases that speak to you in a special way. Type Romans 12:9–21 on a narrow, vertical card and use it as a bookmark in your agenda, journal, or Bible, praying that God will help you live this way, through the power of the Holy Spirit.

Journal. In your private journal, record some of the ways that you conform to the culture of the world. Next to each one, place a corollary of how you could instead act in a God-honoring way. Finally, pray about the changes that must occur to make this happen.

Discussion. Remember John Ortberg's illustration that spiritual transformation is like crossing an ocean? Which method have you been using thus far—the rowboat, the raft, or the sailboat? How can you work in partnership with the Trinity to grow in godliness?

If you were chosen to be a candidate on the television show *Extreme Makeover,* what is one thing about your appearance you would want to change? How about your *inner life*? If God told you He would do an extreme makeover on your *soul* (by the way, He did in Romans 12:2), what is one thing you would request?

Spa Treatment. You can have a mini-makeover today! Go to the beauty salon, have a facial, and ask someone you trust to do whatever hairstyle looks best on you. Go shopping with a friend and allow her to choose a new outfit for you. Or go to a local department store makeup counter and have a consultant do your makeup for you. (Be sure to make a purchase.) Any of these small steps can give you courage to make further, more important changes in your life.

CHAPTER 7

Fashioned by God

So, chosen by God for this new life of love,
dress in the wardrobe God picked out for you:
compassion, kindness, humility, quiet strength, discipline.
Be even-tempered, content with second place, quick to forgive an offense.
Forgive as quickly and completely as the Master forgave you.
And regardless of what else you put on, wear love.
It's your basic, all-purpose garment. Never be without it.

—Colossians 3:12–14 MSG

Many years ago, storyteller Hans Christian Andersen told the tale of "The Emperor's New Clothes." This emperor was so fond of fine new clothes that he spent all his money on acquiring them, and clothes meant more to him than anything else. So, one day two con artists posing as weavers decided on a scheme to swindle him of his money.

They declared that they could make the most magnificent cloth that one could imagine; cloth of the most beautiful colors and elaborate patterns. Not only was the material so beautiful, but the clothes made from it had the special power of being invisible to everyone who was stupid or not fit for his post. . . .

So the Emperor gave the swindlers large sums of money and the two weavers set up their looms in the palace. They demanded the finest thread of the best silk and the finest gold and they pretended to work at their looms. But they put nothing on the looms. The frames stood empty. The silk and gold thread they stuffed into their bags. So they sat pretending to weave, and continued to work at the empty loom till late into the night. Night after night they went home with their money and their bags full of the finest silk and gold thread. Day after day they pretended to work.

When the emperor wanted a progress report, he sent his old minister to check on the weavers. But the minister saw nothing on the looms. Afraid he would be declared stupid or unfit for his post, he raved about the seemingly beautiful fabric. Later, another official was sent to check on the clothes and experienced the same, sinking feeling of wondering why he could perceive nothing when everyone was talking about their beauty. So he, too, faked it and praised the weavers to the emperor, making him very eager to receive his new wardrobe. To his shock, there was nothing there, but he couldn't let on.

"What can this mean?" said the Emperor to himself. "This is terrible. Am I so stupid? Am I not fit to be Emperor? This is disastrous," he thought. But aloud he said, "Oh, the cloth is perfectly wonderful. It has a splendid pattern and such charming colors." And he nodded his approval and smiled appreciatively and stared at the empty looms. He would not, he could not, admit he saw nothing, when his two ministers had praised the material so highly.

When it was time to try on the clothes, the swindlers exclaimed, "The whole suit is as light as a spider's web. Why, you might almost feel as if you had nothing on, but that is just the beauty of it." "Magnificent," cried the ministers, but they could see nothing at all. Indeed there was nothing to be seen. "Now if Your Imperial Majesty would graciously consent to take off your clothes," said the weavers, "we could fit on the new ones." So the Emperor laid aside his clothes and the swindlers pretended to help him piece by piece into the new ones they were supposed to have made. The Emperor turned from side to side in front of the long glass as if admiring himself.

No one, including the Emperor, was willing to see the reality of the situation. And so the Emperor—fully naked but having talked himself into believing he was sporting fine clothing—set off on a grand procession through the town.

>All the people standing by and at the windows cheered and cried, "Oh, how splendid are the Emperor's new clothes. What a magnificent train! How well the clothes fit!" No one dared to admit that he couldn't see anything, for who would want it to be known that he was either stupid or unfit for his post?
>
>But among the crowds a little child suddenly gasped out, "But he hasn't got anything on." And the people began to whisper to one another what the child had said. "He hasn't got anything on." "There's a little child saying he hasn't got anything on." Till everyone was saying, "But he hasn't got anything on." The Emperor himself had the uncomfortable feeling that what they were whispering was only too true. "But I will have to go through with the procession," he said to himself.[1]

That *is* how the story ends. Even when he realized his vanity had precipitated this great deceit, the emperor was far too proud to admit it and put on real clothes. He preferred to be humiliated and proceed with a lie than to humble himself and admit he had been duped. His love of clothing had gotten him into great trouble, for he cared more about that than his people or his kingdom.

> *Don't go shopping for fresh versions of old clothes. You have a new body; you are now fashioned by God.*

I, too, found myself consumed with clothes some years ago. Not because I loved them and not because they looked so great on me, but because I had a hard time finding clothes that fit, and that filled my mind with worry. My automatic response whenever I walked into a store, always a specialty shop for plus-sized women, was to go to the far right of each display, where the largest sizes were. But sometimes I still struck out since some stores went only up to 3X. However, if I was lucky enough to find my size, I would purchase whatever was there. If it was loose and flowing, all the better.

In some ways, I was like the emperor, finding it hard to admit to myself what everyone else could clearly see. My outside didn't match who I was inside. I was using fashion as camouflage, and it wasn't working. So what *do* we present to the world once we've been changed from inside out? What appears during the big-reveal fashion show?

If each of us is created in the image of our Creator, we are truly fashioned by God. We're new, we're transformed. The old wardrobe no longer fits, and God desires to clothe us in His righteousness. "I greatly rejoice in the LORD, I exult in my God; for He has clothed me with the garments of salvation and wrapped me in a robe of righteousness, as a bridegroom wears a turban and as a bride adorns herself with her jewels" (Isa. 61:10).

We've been redesigned. In Colossians 3:3, we read, "For you have died, and your life is hidden with the Messiah in God." Whether or not we look different on the outside, we are always changing on the inside, God is reshaping us, and every day we discover the old world and the old wardrobe don't fit.

Earlier in Colossians Paul addressed a heresy in the church at Colossae that was similar to gnosticism. While gnostics valued knowledge, Paul said knowledge was valuable only when it led to a changed life and right living. In other words, we can know all about God, the Bible, and the walk of faith. We can pray and consider ourselves in close relationship to Jesus Christ, but if our knowledge doesn't direct us into a radical lifestyle, we haven't gone far enough.

"For this reason also, since the day we heard this, we haven't stopped praying for you. We are asking that you may be filled with the knowledge of His will in all wisdom and spiritual understanding, so that you may walk worthy of the Lord, fully pleasing [to Him], bearing fruit in every good work and growing in the knowledge of God. May you be strengthened with all power, according to His glorious might, for all endurance and patience, with joy giving thanks to the Father, who has enabled you to share in the saints' inheritance in the light" (Col. 1:9–12).

Being redesigned doesn't necessarily mean we are a pretty sight. My current body, for instance, has lots of souvenirs from my old lifestyle—not the least of which is sagging skin. Believe me, the word for undergarments—foundation—has taken on a whole new meaning! I thank the Lord every day for the invention of spandex.

But I am redesigned. My shape is different, and all my comfortable former clothing no longer fits. This is quite similar to our spiritual lives as we are being transformed, as daily we are seeking to conform more and more to the image of Christ. "You took off your former way of life, the old man that is corrupted by deceitful desires; you are being renewed in the spirit of your minds; you put on the new man, the one created according to God's [likeness] in righteousness and purity of the truth" (Eph. 4:22–24).

OK, I'll admit it; one of my favorite television shows is *What Not to Wear.* Two fashionistas named Clinton and Stacy invade an unsuspecting person's closet and literally throw out everything she loves and wears. Then they show her three mannequins modeling the kind of outfits she should be wearing. They point out colors, styles, lines, and textures that will best compliment her body and her lifestyle. They give her a $5,000 credit card and send her on a shopping spree to purchase a whole new wardrobe. On her own.

Now that sounds great, doesn't it? That much money to spend on a new wardrobe! But we television viewers watch this fashion victim struggle that first day with wanting to use the money to buy newer and nicer versions of what she always used to wear, rather than the new and more appropriate styles suggested by the experts. Which, of course, brings us to the second day of shopping when the advisers appear at the store and force her to get serious about their new guidelines. She eventually does this—after a fashion, so to speak—and the end result is a new look and the confidence that goes with it.

When I watch this show, I can't help but imagine the apostle Paul going through my spiritual wardrobe and tossing all my favorites in the garbage can. ("Please, no, not my *impatience* sweater. Don't take my *anger* jeans!") I know just what he'd say as he'd pull them one by one from my closet. "Therefore, put to death whatever in you is worldly: sexual immorality, impurity, lust, evil desire, and greed, which is idolatry. . . . and you once walked in these things when you were living in them. But now you must also put away all the following: anger, wrath, malice, slander, and filthy language from your mouth" (Col. 3:5, 7–8).

In other words, don't go shopping for fresh versions of old clothes. You have a new body; you are now fashioned by God. "Do not lie to one another, since you have put off the old man with his practices and have put on the new man, who is being renewed in knowledge according to the image of his Creator" (Col. 3:9–10). How strange would it be if I kept shopping at plus-sized stores if I no longer wore that size? Wouldn't it be crazy to cling to my old wardrobe when I could be wearing a new one fitted to my new size?

Ephesians 4 gives further "fashion" guidelines: "Since you put away lying, speak the truth," (v. 25a). "No rotten talk should come from your mouth" (v. 29a). "All bitterness, anger and wrath, insult and slander must be removed from you, along with all wickedness" (v. 31). And then in Ephesians 5, "But sexual immorality and any impurity or greed should not even be heard of among you, as is proper for saints" (v. 3). In other words, these don't fit the new you! "And coarse and foolish talking or crude joking are not suitable, but rather giving thanks" (v. 4).

I'm sure these are enough lists to have certainly stepped on everyone's toes! By now, you're probably thinking I've gone from preaching to meddling. But it really doesn't matter what you think about *my* words. It only matters what God says, and these mandates are straight from *His* Word.

No, He doesn't only touch on the biggies; He wants to make sure our wardrobes of greed, anger, and even off-color language go right into the trash can. They simply don't fit our new lives.

This is not only a decision when we first trust Christ as our Lord and Savior and experience salvation. This is a conscious commitment to seek godliness each day of our lives. There is no way I can stay a healthy size unless I deliberately consider each day what I eat and how much I move. Such as, by parking my car farther from my destination than in the closest spot and walking extra steps. Or walking up the stairs, not taking the elevator. By ordering smaller portions when I eat out and using a salad plate instead of a dinner plate when at home. I can't coast with my redesigned body; I must make daily choices for health and fitness.

"Kate's Closet" is one practical way Christian women are encouraging a fresh start by providing new wardrobes for recently released female prisoners. This Montgomery, Alabama, boutique is the first stop for those released from nearby Julia Tutwiler Prison. Volunteers welcome each woman with a hug and a smile, then help them choose outfits, complete with accessories—shoes, handbags, and jewelry—for their new lives and job interviews. Each visitor receives new undergarments and panty hose purchased with donated funds. Volunteer makeup artists also give them a makeover with donated Mary Kay cosmetics.

One of the ninety former inmates who have had their appearance transformed in this first year alone, Angela, said the experience is like shopping at a mall except "there's a lot of love at Kate's Closet. It's not just the clothes—it's also God's love, as well as the love and guidance that come from all the volunteers there."

Kim Bullard, the founder, knows this fashion makeover goes hand in hand with the spiritual makeover God is providing for these women. "'Often the women come into "Kate's Closet" seeking what they can get out of it,' Kim says, 'Then they leave thinking about what they can give back. The change in attitude from the time the women come in until the time they walk out the door is amazing . . . and humbling. Prayer and love make all the difference.' She smiles as she adds, 'They come in to get something to wear, and they leave with hope.'"[2]

In my own experience sizing down, I admit that shopping for new clothes can be a lot more fun than I expected. Unfortunately, I was stuck in a bad habit. I'd invariably gravitate toward bulky items, long skirts, and loose fitting everything. That's what I was used to—the bigger the better.

What a revelation to discover that some people actually buy clothes that *fit!* I mean, the sleeves end at the wrist and the shoulders are on the shoulders. You may laugh, but I had to change my whole mind-set. I didn't even wear pants in public until recently!

For our newly redesigned selves, God provides a brand-new wardrobe, and it's a perfect fit! He gives us the guidelines, and then we go shopping and it's up to us. No Clinton or Stacy waiting in the wings to interrupt. "Therefore, God's chosen ones, holy and loved, put on heartfelt compassion, kindness, humility, gentleness, and patience, accepting one another and forgiving one another if anyone has a complaint against another. Just as the Lord has forgiven you, so also you must [forgive]. Above all, [put on] love—the perfect bond of unity" (Col. 3:12–14).

Finding the right fit means giving up comparing ourselves to others. To this day I cannot look at another woman and guess her size because for so many years everyone else's size seemed to me to be . . . well, small. We have to guard against comparisons. All of us have positive and negative points about the way we look. And it's especially hard for those with physical disabilities.

Joni Eareckson Tada, a quadriplegic for more than forty-five years and one of my spiritual heroes, struggled for many years comparing herself with friends when they went shopping together. "We were the same size, but Sheryl's clothes always fit her so well, while mine bunched around my hips because I sat in the wheelchair. Frankly, I couldn't even compare myself to a store window mannequin and come out winning; clothes fit them well because they stood up.

"Viewing myself beside Sheryl in a full-length dressing room mirror taught me quickly about the dangers of comparing myself to others. Yardsticks have a way of robbing us of joy, trapping us in self-pity, and distorting our view of a fair God."[3]

Most of us simply take it for granted that we will eventually find clothes that fit us, whether we have to resort to a specialty shop or not. But increasingly there are those who must have specially adaptive clothing. Limited mobility, Alzheimer's, incontinence, a stroke, a wheelchair, osteoporosis, arthritis, and vision loss all provide special challenges in clothes shopping.

If you need Velcro closures instead of buttons or items that open along the back instead of being pulled over your head, it's hard to find suitable clothing. Julia Buck, a nursing home administrator in Seattle, watched her patients stay in bathrobes and johnnies all day because they couldn't find clothing they could manage on their own. Knowing this affected their self-esteem and compromised their independence, Julia founded her own design company, Buck & Buck clothing.

Adaptive clothing has to be practical, washable, and durable, but it doesn't have to look different. "'How you look affects how you feel. People don't lose their personal sense of style because they've got a disability,'" said Buck.[4]

Years ago, I read "Ragman," a wonderful allegorical story by creative writer Walter Wangerin. A man follows a ragman as he walks the city alleys, coming into contact with many street people. When he comes on a crying woman, he offers to exchange his rags for her handkerchief. On receiving hers, he begins to cry, but she is now left with a clean linen cloth and no tears. Then he comes on a girl whose head is wrapped in a bloody cloth. When he gives her a clean, new yellow bonnet, he takes her rags and soon begins to bleed from his head while also sobbing uncontrollably. Encountering an amputee, he gives him a new coat, in which each sleeve is filled with an arm. But when the ragman takes the old coat, he is suddenly one-armed. Almost stumbling over a drunk, he covers him with a new blanket and takes the old blanket himself. So now the ragman is a pitiful sight and staggers drunkenly, one-armed, head bleeding, and sobbing toward the landfill at the edge of the city. Yet everyone he encountered is now whole.

The narrator of the story, the witness to the ragman's exchanges, watches him die in the dump and then sleeps for days. When he awakens, he is startled to see the ragman standing up whole again. Besides the scar on his forehead, he is healthy and all the rags are now clean and new.

"Well, then I lowered my head and trembling for all that I had seen, I myself walked up to the Ragman. I told him my name with shame, for I was a sorry figure next to him. Then I took off all my clothes in that place, and I said to him with dear yearning in my voice: 'Dress me.'

"He dressed me. My Lord, he put new rags on me, and I am a wonder beside him. The Ragman, the Ragman, the Christ!"[5]

This same "Ragman" - Jesus Christ - promises to take care of us, whatever our fashion need. We can trust Him, and we can be delivered from hiding behind our clothes. Not only does He provide, He also challenges us to have a new perspective. "And why do you worry about clothes? Learn how the wildflowers of the field grow: they don't labor or spin thread. Yet I tell you that not even Solomon in all his splendor was adorned like one of these! If that's how God clothes the grass of the field, which is here today and thrown into the furnace tomorrow, won't He do much more for you—you of little faith? So don't worry, saying, 'What will we eat?' or 'What will we drink?' or 'What will we wear?' For the idolaters eagerly seek all these things, and your heavenly Father knows that you need them" (Matt. 6:28–32).

Spiritual Personal Assessment

Scripture. Read Colossians 3 and underline those qualities you must "take off" as well as those you must now "put on."

Journal. Looking at the wardrobe God has picked out for you (see Colossians 3), what do you think will be the hardest garment for you to "fit" into? (e.g., "discipline because I have no willpower") Write this down and then write a prayer to God to help you in this makeover.

Discussion. What are you "wearing" that God wants to strip from your life? What habits or actions are weighing you down like an ill-fitting set of clothes?

On the television show *What Not to Wear*, the candidate greets her family and friends with a brand-new style. If you were to do this spiritually, what would you hope others would notice most about your deeper walk with Christ?

Spa Treatment. Go on a shopping expedition for . . . new underwear! Yes, go to a shop where there is someone trained to help you get a perfect fit. Then treat yourself to at least one set of lingerie. Try undergarments with spandex, which helps to hold everything in and provides a slimmer appearance. You will be amazed how much better your clothes look when you have foundations that fit properly. Plus, you'll feel more confident in nice lingerie. (Some readers may think this sounds superficial, but I still highly recommend it as a self-esteem booster. And that can only help us, right?)

CHAPTER 8

Comfortable in My Own Skin

> *Don't be concerned about the outward beauty*
> *that depends on fancy hairstyles, expensive jewelry,*
> *or beautiful clothes. You should be known for the beauty*
> *that comes from within, the unfading beauty of a gentle*
> *and quiet spirit, which is so precious to God. That is the*
> *way the holy women of old made themselves beautiful.*
>
> —1 PETER 3:3–5 NLT

On my spa girlfriend getaway day, my final treatment was having my makeup done. For the first time in my life, someone who actually knew something was going to show me how to accentuate my best features and camouflage the rest. I couldn't wait.

"The kind of foundation this face needs is the heavy coverage, you know, kind of like spackling!" I exclaimed as Jill gathered the tools of her trade.

"Actually, what I like to do is prepare your own unique foundation that exactly matches your skin so that no one can tell it's there," she replied.

Now that's a novel idea—*enhance* rather than *cover up*. So Jill mixed various concoctions and emerged with my tailor-made foundation. And she was right. Once she had deftly applied it with a sponge (no messy fingers here), I looked in the mirror and it was . . . me. A smoother complexion that—dare I say it—actually *glowed.*

The session continued as she applied blush, eye makeup, and lip liner. Soon I was ready to go and wow the folks back home. My husband and teenage daughter both kept looking at me and commenting on how great I looked. But not fake. I guess that's what a great aesthetician does—makes you look just like yourself, only more so.

Needless to say, I purchased my "signature foundation" and have since tried to emulate Jill's makeup skills. I'm doing OK, with only occasional forays into the Tammy Faye school of cosmetology.

This then, is the true message of God's spa treatment of His children. He wants to do all He can to *enhance who we already are,* to uncover our hearts and souls so that we can shine in freedom and verity. We have been so caught up in covering our imperfections that we have forgotten to build on our strengths. Just as the best makeup job is one in which you don't look made-up, the best spa for your soul is one in which God heals, massages, cleanses, and beautifies from the inside out.

I always wanted to be beautiful—to be *beautiful for God* even. I hoped and prayed that God would use me as a perfect example of exquisite beauty—a Ming vase for Him. But, alas, I discovered early on that I was not a Ming vase but merely a clay pot, full of cracks and imperfections and broken in several places. Ordinary in many ways. Or, as my eldest son once described me in his youth, "just a regular old lady!"

Today I embrace the beauty of this very fact, because I know God has chosen to use me as a woman who is not grand, lofty, and intimidatingly beautiful. If others draw any appeal from me at all it is through my down-to-earth qualities. I'm the woman next door. If God can work in *me* and through *me,* there's hope for everyone!

The apostle Paul taught this two thousand years ago. Listen to his words in 2 Corinthians 4:7–8, 16: "Now we have this treasure in clay jars, so that this extraordinary power may be from God and not from us. We are pressured in every way but not crushed; we are perplexed but not in despair; . . . Therefore we do not give up; even though our outer person is being destroyed, our inner person is being renewed day by day."

My California friend Nancy Stafford *is* actually beautiful, and though she is an accomplished actor and former beauty queen, God is using her inner beauty today in furthering His kingdom. In *Beauty by the Book: Seeing Yourself as God Sees You,* she reminds us, "Real beauty isn't what we see in magazines or on movie screens and it doesn't depend on the opinions of others or the changing tastes of culture. True beauty is seeing ourselves as God sees us, reflected in the mirror of His word."[1]

We know that God sees us as beautiful, "and the king will desire your beauty. Bow down to him, for he is your lord" (Ps. 45:11). "That means captivated, smitten, fascinated, spellbound and delighted. . . . Enthralled is how God in heaven feels about you. He is taken with you. Undistracted. Intensely interested. Emotionally connected. He enjoys your laughter and takes pleasure in the way you think. He is not bored with you, and He would never consider you ordinary. There is no way you will ever go unnoticed with God. You are beautiful to Him. Incredibly, breathtakingly beautiful."[2]

If we can ever truly experience this kind of love and acceptance and empowering from our heavenly Father, we can finally become comfortable in our own skin.

I'm growing into that phrase—being comfortable in my own skin. I've lived long enough now to have weathered some failures in life and celebrated a few successes as well. But I wouldn't trade my current seasoned mind for a twenty-year-old body. I've paid too high a price for my knowledge and wisdom not to embrace it fully.

Speaking of skin, time and gravity have taken over mine and any day now I expect someone to suggest I straighten my panty hose when I'm not actually wearing any! So what if this body will never wear a bikini again? I'm determined to always swim when I get the chance without worrying about how I look in a bathing suit. Life is far too short to stay out of the water because of self-consciousness!

Author Anne Lamott who is "fifty plus change" shared that "I still have terrible moments when I despair about my body—time and gravity have not made various parts of it higher and firmer. But those are just moments now—I used to have *years* when I believed I was more beautiful if I jiggled less, if all parts of my body stopped moving when I did. But I know two things now that I didn't at thirty: That when we get to heaven, we will discover that the appearance of our butts and our skin was 127th on the list of what mattered on this earth. And that I am not going to live forever. Knowing these things has "set me free."

Age has given me what I was looking for my entire life—it has given me *me*. It has provided time and experience and failures and triumphs and time-tested friends who have helped me step into the shape that was waiting for me. I fit into me now. I have an organic life, finally, not necessarily the one people imagined for me, or tried to get me to have. I have the life I longed for. I have become the woman I hardly dared imagine I could be. . . . And as that old saying goes, it's not that I think less of myself, but that I think of myself less often. And that feels like heaven to me."[3]

Now that you're finishing *Refresh!*, are you ready to embrace the beauty God has given you? Yes, *you!* And *me!* You see, we were each made in the image of God and beauty is in our essence. So stop covering up and let your true self shine through. Be comfortable with who you are and discover more each day why God has put you here on earth at this time. He intends to use you and grow you into an exciting and adventurous woman of faith.

Angela Thomas spent much of her life bemoaning the fact that she was ordinary. When she went through a devastating divorce, it was even harder to accept that God saw her as beautiful. But in her book *Do You Think I'm Beautiful?* she stated, "When God looks into the eyes of a woman, He sees all the beauty He created there. He sees every potential and gift. He sees what can be and redeems what has been. He loves the curly hair that you wish were straight. He is taken with your smile and the shape of your nose. He's crazy about big feet and knobby knees and every curve that is particular to you. He is the One who loves the inside and outside of you. You were all His idea, and you are physically and emotionally beautiful to Him."[4]

Years ago I was relieved to receive via email a digital picture of my then twenty-five-year-old daughter, Fiona, who is beautiful and rarely wears makeup. In fact, at that time she was living in a small village in Guinea, West Africa, where it is often 100 degrees in the shade, so makeup would probably melt anyway. Communication was hard because in that country electricity was rare. Since this was the first photo in months, I found myself staring at her all day, grateful that she looked healthy and happy!

Fiona also has an impressive intellect and could be doing anything with her life, but she chose to serve with the Peace Corps in a desperately poor Muslim country, helping men and women start small businesses so they can be self-sufficient. Now, after receiving her master's degree in international development from the London School of Economics, she is overseas helping set up some international development programs.

I'm proud of her (as I am of all my children and their various pursuits). I have moments of anxiety for her – moments I try to channel into prayer. But I am not surprised at Fiona's choices. Since she was a little girl, Fiona has been comfortable in her own skin. Early in life she discovered her strengths and decided to focus on what was most important. Very few things rattle her now, and I've learned from her not to sweat the small stuff.

Christian mystic Julian of Norwich once said, "And all manner of things will be well." John and Stasi Eldredge, in their book *Captivating*, agreed. "Every woman has a beauty to unveil. She doesn't have to conjure it, go get it from a salon, have plastic surgery or breast implants. No, beauty is an essence given to every woman at her creation. So this is what it's like to be with a woman at rest, a woman comfortable in her feminine beauty. She is enjoyable to be with. She is lovely. In her presence your heart stops holding its breath. You relax and believe once again that all will be well. And this is also why a woman who is striving is so disturbing, for a woman who is not at rest in her heart says to the world, *All is not well. Things are not going to turn out all right.*"[5]

God wants us to be at rest in our hearts, to be comfortable in the way He made us. "For man sees what is visible, but the LORD sees the heart" (1 Sam. 16:7b).

> *He is the One who loves the inside and outside of you. You were all His idea, and you are physically and emotionally beautiful to Him.*
>
> —ANGELA THOMAS

I can think of at least one beauty in the Bible who was definitely comfortable in her own skin— comfortable enough to risk her life in doing the right thing. I'm speaking of Esther, who lived five hundred years before Christ. You may remember her as the Jewish orphan who lived with her cousin and adopted father, Mordecai, exiled in Persia during the reign of King Xerxes. The first time we read of Esther, it is revealed that she "had a beautiful figure and was extremely good-looking" (Esther 2:7b). In other words, she was a knockout.

When Xerxes was looking for a new queen and held a beauty contest to find her, Esther won hands down. First, she impressed Hegai, the eunuch in charge of the harem. He could tell she was not only beautiful on the outside but also held inner beauty. So much so that "he accelerated the process of the beauty treatments and the special diet that she received. He assigned seven hand-picked female servants to her from the palace and transferred her and her servants to the harem's best quarters" (Esther 2:9b)

But before she could be presented to the king, she had to undergo a beauty spa for a whole year—"beauty treatments with oil of myrrh for six months and then with perfumes and cosmetics for [another] six months" (Esther 2:12b). If she was a beauty before, imagine how she looked afterward! When the king saw Esther, it was love at first sight and he immediately crowned her the new queen of Persia. Esther went from a poor, orphaned exile to queen and wife of the most powerful man in the known world, all because of a pretty face and an even prettier heart. However, since the former queen, Vashti, had been banished for acting uppity, Esther knew she needed to play it safe, keeping her Jewish heritage a secret and also not barging in on the king unless summoned first.

But this story had eternal ramifications as well.

A long time before Esther, God had made a promise to a man named Abraham. That promise was to bless all the nations through his seed and bring God's son to the world through his bloodline, because of Abraham's faithfulness. The Jews are the direct descendants of Abraham and were endangered of becoming extinct as the book of Esther unfolds. In order for the Messiah to enter the world through the Jewish nation, the Jewish nation must be preserved, and that is exactly where Esther comes into the picture. In her story we see loyalty, wisdom, humility, obedience, kindness, and discretion from Esther's character, as well as, bravery, concern for others above herself, prudence, and trust and faithfulness in her God. God used these qualities contained in the character of Esther to confront the enemy, approach the throne, and reverse a death sentence to a nation. It is this reversal that enabled God's promise to Abraham so long ago to be fulfilled with the eventual birth, death, and resurrection of Jesus, His Son.[6]

When Esther came to the throne, trouble was stirring in the kingdom in the form of Haman, one of King Xerxes' top nobles. Haman was furious that Mordecai would not bow down to him, and he plotted to destroy Mordecai and all the Jews, little knowing that his queen was one of them. In desperation, Mordecai asked Esther to intervene on behalf of her people even though it meant risking the king's wrath. "Who knows, perhaps you have come to the kingdom for such a time as this" (Esther 4:14b).

Esther requested that her people join her and her maids in prayer and fasting. She knew she had limited power as the queen, but she also knew she had *unlimited* power as a daughter of the true God. "Charm is deceptive and beauty is fleeting, but a woman who fears the LORD will be praised" (Prov. 31:30). Because of this, Esther felt secure in pursuing what she believed to be God's mission. "'I will go to the king even if it is against the law. If I perish, I perish'" (Esther 4:16b). Even though the word "God" is never mentioned in this book of the Bible, He is clearly present from start to finish.

The king welcomed Esther and even gave her two banquets that she used to expose Haman as the initiator of a plot to annihilate the Jews. As a result of her courage and quick intellect, the Jews were delivered and Haman and all his family were killed, their land handed over to Esther and Mordecai.

Both Mordecai and Esther were so grateful to God for His faithfulness that they sent letters to the Jews in all the provinces in Persia instructing them to celebrate the two days of their deliverance every year. They called it the feast of Purim, from the word *pur,* meaning "lot" or "dice." Haman had cast lots to determine the day the Jews should die (see Esther 3:7; 9:24, 26). God turned it to a day of victory, and they were grateful to Him for deliverance. The Jewish people still celebrate Purim as a lasting memorial to God's faithfulness.

Somehow it doesn't seem too farfetched to believe that Esther experienced a spa for her soul as well as her beauty spa in preparation for her time at the palace. If she had been merely outwardly beautiful, it's unlikely she would have had the courage and willingness to intervene in the affairs of state. In addition to being prepared, her heart also was willing to respond when God's call came. Are *you* willing?

Perhaps you don't feel particularly beautiful, queenly, or qualified, but if you are following Christ and seeking to obey His will and His way, there will be innumerable opportunities for you to make a difference in this world. The more we seek His face, the more like Him we become as the King adopts us as His very own. If you approach God with a request, He can use your inner beauty—as He used Esther's—to confront an enemy and thwart an evil plan. Who knows whether you have not attained royalty for such a time as this?

Spiritual Personal Assessment

Scripture. Read the entire book of Esther and underline insights you gain from her actions of courage and faith. Look for evidences of God and His working throughout this story, even though He is never mentioned.

Journal. List the most beautiful women you know (or know of). Now, next to each name, write why you think they are beautiful. This may be because of outer or inner qualities. Review your list and examine your perceptions of beauty. Do they align with what God says in 1 Peter 3:3–5?

Discussion. Are you "comfortable in your feminine beauty" (Eldredge), or do you find it awkward to embrace the beauty God has given you, both outer and inner? If so, why? What is one step you could take today to enhance rather than camouflage your beauty?

Anne Lamott said, "I fit into me now. . . . It's not that I think less of myself, but that I think of myself less often." Do you feel comfortable in your own skin, or are you still trying to be someone else? What would it take for you to embrace the person God created you to be, rather than the one everyone else expects you to be? Ask God to help you on that path.

Spa Treatment. As you finish *Refresh!,* indulge in beauty as a ministry to your soul. Think of the things that speak to your heart. It might be the beauty of nature. If so, I encourage you to plan an outing to nearby botanical gardens or a nature preserve or a drive to the coast. Take materials that will help you be comfortable in relaxing there and soaking up beauty that touches your heart. Others might find beauty at a Victorian tea parlor with its crisp linen tablecloths and fine china. Dress up and reserve a table alone where you can sip hot tea, eat delicate scones, and listen to classical music. There are many different ways to absorb beauty. Only you know what speaks to you. But remember as you go on your outing that God is the Creator of all beauty. He loves you more than you can imagine! Savor it. Relish it. Bask in beauty and know you are part of the beauty around you.

He Restores My Soul

"He leads me beside still waters. He restores my soul."
—PSALM 23:2-3

The year is brand new as I walk around the small freshwater pond in the midst of Texas hill country. Today I've gladly traded in New England snow for a warm January at Round Top Retreat. Once again I settle down "beside still waters" for a spa for my soul. This time, however, I am not alone.

Twenty other Christian sisters have joined me for a refreshing week of rest, recreation and renewal before embarking on this new year of ministry. We are all speakers and authors and some of us have never even been to a retreat where we were not *the* speaker, *the* director or *the* worship leader! Until now. Here we are all just peers and can simply share our lives and dreams in authentic, vulnerable ways -knowing the others will understand and keep confidences.

Our focus this week is on *being*, not *doing* — in fact we have deliberately left behind the internet, self-promotion and all business transactions. No one is here to impress anyone else.

Friends at First Place 4 Health are investing in us so that we might touch the world in Christ's name. Their program emphasizes a balanced life in four major health areas: physical, mental, emotional and spiritual. And so we strategize with dietitians, exercise therapists, life coaches, nutritionists and nurses (for all the medical tests). But mostly we share from the heart as we soak up God's love and the support of our fellow SpaSisters.

We all have areas of health we need to address. Some of us need to lose weight and at least one of us hopes to gain weight (imagine that). We all want to learn better ways of eating healthy in the midst of traveling and exercising regularly in the midst of so much time writing on computers. But that covers just the physical. We also share and address goals in the mental, emotional and spiritual realms….and in the process of laughing and crying, souls are knit together.

Carole closes our week by encouraging us to "Give God a Year – Change Your Life Forever!" and we spend quiet time prayerfully writing down goals and 'impossible' prayers for such life changes. Next year, Lord willing, we will all gather here again to see what God has done.*

As I fly home to the frigid Northeast I reflect on our changing world and the particular challenges facing all of us in this new year. As is my tradition, I have chosen a special verse for this new year – one that I believe God wants to use to both encourage and exhort me with as my days unfold. This year it is from Jeremiah 17:7-8 "Blessed is the man who trusts in the Lord, whose confidence indeed is the Lord. He will be like a tree planted by water: it sends its roots out toward a stream, it doesn't fear when heat comes, and its foliage remains green. It will not worry in a year of drought or cease producing fruit."

As I seek God to restore my soul, I must remember that He is the One who nourishes us even (and perhaps especially) during times of heat and drought. If we make a deliberate decision to *trust the Lord* and *make Him our hope and confidence*, then He offers us the 'health by water' *spa*. These verses suggest to me that maintaining *deep roots* in the solid and biblical foundation of faith is a must. Also, being *planted by water* is key – daily drawing close to Jesus Christ who is indeed the Living Water. The One who truly refreshes.

Will you remember these things as times of loss, concern, change or dryness come your way? Trust Him to guide and provide in every situation and then you will reap the benefits. What are they? The verse says we will *not worry when things are difficult* and we *will never cease to bear fruit that will last.*

Thank you for journeying with me through the many "spa treatments" in *Refresh!* as we have sought together to find balance in our lives so that we indeed might be all God created us to be — whole, healed, empowered and healthy! Remember that this is an ongoing process and that you are not alone.

> **Rest in God alone, my soul, for my hope comes from Him.**
> PSALM 62.5

*First Place 4 Health offers this kind of "Wellness Week" each year for anyone who would like to participate. Go to their website for more information www.FirstPlace4Health.com.

Notes

~ 🌺 ~

Prologue—Beside Still Waters

1. Max Lucado, *Come Thirsty* (Nashville, Tenn.: W Publishing Group, a division of Thomas Nelson, Inc. 2004), 12.

Chapter 1—Come Apart Awhile

1. Lindsey O'Connor, *If Mama Goes South, We're All Going with Her* (Grand Rapids, Mich.: Revell, 2003), 212–13.

2. Alice Gray and Steve Stephens, *The Worn Out Woman* (Sisters, Ore.: Multnomah), 126.

3. Lynne M. Baab, *Sabbath Keeping* (Downers Grove, Ill.: InterVarsity, 2005), 11.

4. Ibid., 90.

5. Henri Nouwen, quoted by Paula Rinehart in "Love: Delighting in God's Tenderness," *Discipleship Journal* 114 (November/December 1999).

6. Lynne M. Baab, *A Renewed Spirituality* (Downers Grove, Ill.: InterVarsity, 2002), 170.

7. Anne Morrow Lindbergh, *Gift from the Sea* (New York: Random House, 1951).

8. Laura Shaffer, "Two's Company," *Discipleship Journal* (March/April 2005), 75–76.

Chapter 2—Deep Cleansing

1. Cynthia Spell Humbert, *Deceived by Shame, Desired by God* (Colorado Springs, Colo.: NavPress, 2001), 27–28.

2. Ibid., 46.

3. Jennifer Kennedy Dean, *He Restores My Soul* (Nashville, Tenn.: B & H Publishing Group, 1999) 57-58.

Chapter 3—The Master's Massage

1. Paula Rinehart, "Good Enough—Are You Tired of Trying to Measure Up?" *Discipleship Journal* (September 1998).

2. James I. Packer, *Knowing God* (Downers Grove, Ill.: InterVarsity, 1973).

3. Brenda Waggoner, *The Velveteen Woman* (Colorado Springs, Colo.: Cook, 1999), 28.

Chapter 4—Body Image

1. Found at www.wellesley.edu/Health/BodyImage/media/html.

2. Deborah Newman, *Comfortable in Your Own Skin* (Wheaton, Ill.: Tyndale, 2007), 23.

3. Lynne M. Baab, *A Renewed Spirituality* (Downers Grove, Ill.: InterVarsity, 2002), 193–94.

4. Newman, *Loving Your Body*, 98.

5. Randy Robison, "Slimming Down the Body of Christ," *Today's Christian Woman* (January/February 2005), 22.

6. Newman, *Loving Your Body*, 169–70.

7. Janet Holm McHenry, "Take a Hike!" *Today's Christian Woman* (March/April 2003), 65.

8. Robison, "Slimming Down the Body of Christ," 24.

9. Elyse Fitzpatrick, *The Afternoon of Life* (Phillipsburg, N.J.: P & R, 2004), 167.

10. Valerie Bell, *She Can Laugh at the Days to Come* (Grand Rapids, Mich.: Zondervan, 1996), 23.

11. Max Lucado, "Temple Talk," *Discipleship Journal* 141 (2004), 53.

12. Ibid.

13. Lael Arrington, "Coping with Chronic Pain," *Focus Over Fifty,* www.family.org/focusoverfifty/justforyou.

14. Karla Worley, "Body Beautiful," *Today's Christian Woman* (March/April 2003).

Chapter 5—Cardiotherapy

1. www.nhlbi.nih.gov/health/hearttruth/events/index.htm.

2. Paula Dranov, "What Even Young Women Need to Know about Heart Disease," *Ladies Home Journal* (February 2005), 170.

3. Christine Gorman, "Broken Heart," *Time* (February 21, 2005).

4. Paula Rinehart, *Strong Women, Soft Hearts* (Nashville, Tenn.: W Publishing Group, 2001), 107.

5. Jessica Shaver, "A Prayer for Freedom," *Virtue* (January/February 1996).

6. Lewis Smedes, *Keeping Hope Alive* (Nashville, Tenn.: Nelson, 1998), 96.

7. Dean Ornish, M.D., *Love and Survival* (New York: HarperCollins, 1998), 28–29.

8.   Kyle Roderick, *Spa* (March/April 2005), 52.

9.   Brent Curtis and John Eldredge, *The Sacred Romance* (Nashville, Tenn.: Nelson, 1997), 6.

10. Ibid., 3.

Chapter 6—Extreme Makeover

1.   Michele Weldon, "Reality TV That Truly Transforms," *Suburban Living* (July/August 2004), 128.

2.   John Ortberg, "True (and False) Transformation," *Leadership Journal* (2002), www.christianitytoday.com/le/2002.

3.   Cynthia Lunceford with Valerie Payne, "Extreme Makeover," *Worldwide Challenge* (November/December 2004), 48.

Chapter 7—Fashioned by God

1.   Hans Christian Andersen, "The Emperor's New Clothes," adapted by Sara and Stephen Corrin in *Stories for Seven-Year-Olds* (London: Faber and Faber, 1989).

2.   Janice Shaw Crouse, "Clothed with Hope," *Today's Christian Woman* (May/June 2004), 56.

3.   Joni Eareckson Tada, "Those Enviable Others," *Partnership* (May/June 1987), 29.

4.   "When You Can No Longer Buy Clothes off the Rack," *Hartford Courant.*

5.   Walter Wangerin Jr., *The Ragman and Other Cries of Faith* (New York: HarperCollins, 1984).

Chapter 8—Comfortable in My Own Skin

1.   Nancy Stafford, *Beauty by the Book: Seeing Yourself as God Sees You* (Sisters, Ore.: Multnomah, 2002), 9.

2. Angela Thomas, *Do You Think I'm Beautiful?* (Nashville, Tenn.: Nelson, 2003), 25.

3. Anne Lamott, *Plan B* (New York: Riverhead/Penguin, 2005), 172–76.

4. Thomas, *Do You Think I'm Beautiful?*, 24.

5. John and Stasi Eldredge, *Captivating* (Nashville, Tenn.: Nelson, 2005), 38.

6. Christy Hesslen, "For Such a Time as This," www.westarkchurchofchrist.org/wings/lbcchristy4.htm.

Acknowledgments

To my husband, Mike, for his willingness to review the manuscript and offer theological comments (even though he definitely declared it a woman's book!), thank you for supporting me in using my gifts not only for our family but also for the kingdom. I am always grateful to my family, who puts up with a lot in order for me to write a book. Thanks, especially, Mike and Maggie, for your patience and willingness to eat takeout during my crunch writing times. Thanks to son Justin who regularly prays for all my writing and speaking, to son Tim and daughter Fiona who graciously gave me the computer on which to write this book, and to daughter Maggie for endless beauty and makeup tips to keep her mama lookin' good!

Thanks, y'all, to my parents, Pratt and Sarah Secrest, for being lifelong encouragers of me and everything I have ever attempted. No matter what my age or stage, you *always* think I'm beautiful. And to my sister Susan Waters, for reading an early copy of this book and declaring it "the best you've written yet." Thanks also to my sister Cathy Ray, who came and helped so much during a time of extreme makeover in my life.

Deep gratitude goes to my dear friend, Maggie Rowe, who prayed daily for this project and who supports and sustains me in innumerable ways. Also my friend Judith Franzen, my "expert" in all things spa related. Judy, your advice and facials and other aesthetician input helped make this a reality. To Karen Memmott and Dana Spicer of Mainly Tea

Parlour, thanks for the beauty and peace that restore my soul there. Thanks to my Daybreak prayer circle—Karen, Jessica, and Judy—for our research spa day!

Thanks to all friends at the *Willowbank* in Bermuda for their ministry to our souls and for offering *Spa for the Soul* retreat to the women of Bermuda.

Each day I keep in touch with my own *SpaSisters* scattered cross country, with whom I share common goals, struggles and ministry. Thanks, dear ones (you know who you are) for our annual time apart at God's feet and in each other's faces. We are in this together and God is the Victor in all our endeavors!

A great word of gratitude to the George and Karen Porter and the folks at Bold Vision Books for making this revised book *Refresh!* a beautiful and exciting reality.

And finally, thanks to the Lover of my soul—Jesus Christ—for His grace and mercy in my life.

Lucinda Secrest McDowell
"Sunnyside"
Wethersfield, Connecticut
January 2016

About the Author

Every word you give me is a miracle word—
how could I help but obey?
Break open your words, let the light shine out,
let ordinary people see the meaning.

—Psalm 119:129–30 MSG

Lucinda Secrest McDowell, M.T.S., has been a storyteller all her life! Her greatest joy is to make God's faithfulness visible and real through practical illustrations of biblical truth in ordinary life. In addition to *Refresh!*, she has authored eleven other books including *Live These Words, Dwelling Places, Role of a Lifetime, Quilts from Heaven*, and *Amazed by Grace*. She is also a contributing author to 25 books and has published in more than 50 magazines, earning Mount Hermon's "Writer of the Year" award. Cindy holds degrees from Gordon-Conwell Theological Seminary and Furman University, and also studied at the Wheaton Graduate School of Communication.

Through her ministry, "Encouraging Words," (www. EncouragingWords.net) she brings enthusiastic wit and wisdom as an international conference speaker and seminar teacher. She is particularly energized by interacting with people to create innovative presentations on special themes. Cindy is privileged to have had a variety of life experiences such as radio producer and broadcaster, editor and journalist for two international conventions, and has directed missions, women's ministries and pastoral care at large churches in both California and Connecticut. In addition to reading, watching and sharing stories, Cindy enjoys tea parties, letters on fine stationery, cozy quilts, soothing massage, good books, country music, bright colors and laughing friends. A southerner from birth, she writes from "Sunnyside" cottage in New England.

For more information on her writing and speaking, contact Cindy at:

Lucinda Secrest McDowell
Encouraging Words That Transform
P.O. Box 290707
Wethersfield CT 06129 USA
cindy@encouragingwords.net
www.EncouragingWords.net
860.402.9551

Twitter - @lucindasmcdowel
Facebook - LucindaSecrestMcDowell

"My mission is to glorify God and live in His grace and freedom, and through the power of the Holy Spirit to use my gifts to communicate God's faithfulness, extend His grace, and encourage others to trust Him fully." —L. S. M.

Made in the USA
Middletown, DE
13 March 2016